D0419161

THE
STATIONERS'
COMPANY

THE
STATIONERS'
COMPANY
1918-1977

A LIVERY COMPANY IN THE MODERN WORLD

PHILIP UNWIN

PUBLISHED BY ORDER OF THE MASTER, WARDENS
AND COURT OF ASSISTANTS OF THE WORSHIPFUL COMPANY
OF STATIONERS AND NEWSPAPER MAKERS

ERNEST BENN LIMITED

LONDON & TONBRIDGE

WESTMINSTER
CITY LIBRARIES

First published 1978 by
Ernest Benn Limited
25 New Street Square, London, EC4A 3JA
& Sovereign Way, Tonbridge, Kent, TN9 1RW

Registered at Stationers' Hall 1978
© *The Worshipful Company of Stationers*
and Newspaper Makers 1978

Printed in Great Britain

ISBN *0 510-00019-3*

7902

DR

338 · 632

24 APR 1978

WESTMINSTER
CITY LIBRARIES

Contents

WESTMINSTER
CITY LIBRARIES

WESTMINSTER
CITY LIBRARIES

Acknowledgements

THE IDEA OF THIS SHORT BOOK originated with Past Master George Riddell and I am greatly indebted to him for his help, advice and constructive criticism. Without his encouragement, and that of David Wyndham-Smith and Peter Rippon details of the work of the Livery Committee would have been a good deal more difficult to trace. I am also most grateful to our recent Masters, Leonard Kenyon and Jack Matson, for help at an early stage, to Christopher Rivington and especially to Patrick Wells (Clerk to the Company 1957–74) for his careful reading of the typescript. Warm thanks are also due to Colonel Rubens, Major John Moon and Dudley Ward for their readiness to search out many of the less accessible facts of our history. In addition, the expert attention of Kenneth Day in preparation of the book for the printers, also, with James Moran, in proof-reading, has accomplished much for the final appearance of my work.

It must also be emphasised that this book owes its publication very largely to those who subscribed for copies in advance, also to Liverymen Eric W. Haylock through whom free paper has been supplied by T. S. Corrigan and The Inveresk Group Limited, to John N. Heyer for binding material likewise, as well as to Jamie Mackay Miller who undertook production at cost. The jacket paper was freely supplied by Michael Chater of Grosvenor Chater & Company Limited. Above all we are indebted to our present Master, E. Glanvill Benn, through whom we received the wonderful overall offer from Liveryman Timothy Benn, on behalf of Benn Brothers Limited, to underwrite the deficit balance on the project and to handle its publication.

January 1978   P.U.

Introduction

THE WORSHIPFUL COMPANY of Stationers and Newspapermakers is one of the largest of the Livery Companies of the City of London and it possesses a Hall of outstanding beauty dating from just after the Great Fire of 1666. It is one of the few Livery Companies in which membership is restricted to those engaged in one of the 'crafts'—on a liberal interpretation—embraced in the trade of Stationer. By Patrimony, also, others are accepted provided that their fathers were Liverymen at the time of the candidate's birth.

In 1960 Cyprian Blagden's *The Stationers' Company* was published and a copy of it is presented to every new Liveryman. It is a full-length study, a work of scholarship, covering more than five centuries and most space was, rightly, devoted to the years from 1560 to 1800 when the Company was enjoying its greatest influence in the control of printers, its one-time monopoly of certain books, and its part in the control of copyright. With so large a span of years to be covered it was possible for only eight pages to be allocated to the activities of the present century, and while, historically, it may have counted for less in recent times, the Company has become increasingly active over the past fifty years—by comparison with its relative somnolence around the turn of the century.

The present short work, by a Past Master of the Company, is intended to serve as a supplement to Mr Blagden's history and it describes ways in which new life has been breathed into an institution which may have appeared, at one time, to have lost its significance and much of the purpose of its existence.

The last page of the earlier book recorded the sale, for a very substantial sum, of the Stationers' bombed property on Ludgate Hill including the former site of Simpkin Marshall, the once famous book wholesalers, and the author expressed the hope

9

that if this were 'invested with imagination and the income used with discretion, if the traditional ties with the book trade are maintained and the recent association with Fleet Street fostered, the Company may be, in the years to come, not only prosperous but once again of service'. The savage inroads of inflation have inevitably—if temporarily—impaired the financial prosperity of the Company, but apart from that one aspect it may fairly be claimed that the greater part of Mr Blagden's aspirations are well on the way to realization; if the Promised Land has not yet been reached, the ship is, at least, headed in the right direction.

Before attempting to describe the many significant developments stemming from the sale of that freehold, it has been thought wise to begin this account with the end of the Great War in 1918. As in so many other spheres of national life, that year became a watershed marking changes of outlook and it can be seen as a time when new ideas, generated by younger men, began to find acceptance by their elders. There was, of course, resistance and progress was far from rapid in Stationers' Hall, but after twenty years substantial advances had been made. Most notably the establishment of the Livery Committee which, under the leadership of J. R. Riddell, then Principal of the St Bride's Foundation Printing School (and father of Dr George Riddell), prepared the way for the increasingly important part now played by the Livery in Company affairs. This is one reason why the present account overlaps to a very small extent the period dealt with in the earlier book and it has been felt that rather more inside detail of the 1920s and 1930s can be of lively interest to present members of the Livery.

The primary aim has been to describe more fully the events since that terrible night in October 1940 when fire bombs destroyed the roof and beautiful ceiling of our Hall and irreparably damaged the Court Room, to be followed by the great City raid of 29-30 December when the properties in Wood Street and on Ludgate Hill—with their rents—were lost to the Company. Renter Wardenship in 1940-41 and service as

Livery Representative nine years later were unforgettable experiences for the author and provided opportunities to observe the working of the Company at first hand in times of exceptional problems.

The end of the Second World War in 1945 found the Company virtually without income and most of its premises unusable, yet once more—as after the previous war—with a valuable number of younger men coming forward to take up the Livery soon after they were released from the Forces. Acute shortage of materials coupled with the inevitable need to give priority to more essential building, delayed for six years the day when a dinner of any sort could once more be served in Stationers' Hall and not until 1957, for the Quatercentenary, were the kitchens sufficiently operational to enable a full-scale Livery Dinner to be held there. Throughout these years, however, interest was kept alive, not least by the Livery Committee who managed, with a certain amount of self-help in those days of rationing, to produce an annual lunch in the rebuilt Court Room.

The establishment of a properly equipped, fire-proof Muniments Room, the gift of a Liveryman, Ellic Howe, enabled the Company's treasures to be appropriately housed under the supervision of the then Master, Sidney Hodgson, a distinguished bookman and head of the famous book auctioneers. He it was who organized, with the help of some Liverymen, an attractive exhibition of our ancient records, in the Stock Room, at the time of the Festival of Britain in 1951.

Financially, the matter of greatest consequence in the 1950s was the sale of the Ludgate Hill freehold for the impressive sum of £663,000. The story behind it and all that has stemmed from the operation, including the various schools of thought in the matter of investment, are of great interest. From that followed the intricate and contentious question of the winding-up of the so-called English Stock of the Company, involving as it did a private Act of Parliament and the creation of the various scales of Annuities for holders of the original Shares— Court, Livery, and Yeomanry.

A few years later came the near-revolutionary step of changing the time-honoured, but not wholly efficient, method of election to the Court, solely on seniority; new provision was made for the election of five new members on Merit and also there was provision for resignation from the Court. An early benefit has been the quite considerable lowering of the average age of the Court Assistants, as well as the great advantage of being able to select, ahead of their seniority in the Livery, somewhat younger men who have given outstanding service to the Company, to the city of London, or to their own Trades.

On the initiative of a former Master, Charles Rivington, a systematic effort was made to trace the Freemen of the Company who, having taken up the Freedom after completion of their apprenticeship, had not proceeded to the Livery. As a result, regular functions are now held for this mainly much younger group in the Company. To Mr Rivington also goes great credit for his invaluable work in the establishment and proper organization of the Company's Library, now well equipped on the floor above the Court Room. Tribute is paid also to the remarkable amount of work accomplished in earlier days by a miniscule staff and a part-time Clerk. The Rivington family supplied Clerks throughout the past century but with the retirement of Reginald T. Rivington in 1957 and the appointment of Patrick Wells there came reorganization and great expansion in the Company's activities, especially after the sale of the property and the extinguishment of the English Stock. Revolutionary changes in the Company's School at Hornsey are described, as is the work of the Charities Committee. Especially interesting to many too is that, more than sixty years since Entry at Stationers' Hall ceased to be a condition of copyright, our Registry is still used every year to record the publication of an astonishing variety of books, pamphlets, songs, etc., which fall outside the mainstream of commercial publishing.

From this book a Liveryman can gain some idea of the experiences open to him over the years from the time when he appears before the Court for the 'Cloathing' ceremony. It concludes with a short chapter on the work of Master and Wardens, with special reference to the many duties and engagements—many of them colourful and enjoyable—which await a Master during his year of office.

CHAPTER ONE

Into the Nineteen-Twenties

WHILE THE DECADE of the 'Twenties was to see the beginnings of important changes in the Stationers' Company, the first stirrings began in that climactic year of 1918. As it dawned, most people on the Home Front, utterly weary of their life with its badly planned rationing, food queues, semi-blackout, general shortages, and the terrible, unending casualty lists from the Western Front, would have found it impossible to visualize what that year was, in fact, to bring forth. Yet, after their gigantic Spring Offensive with its enormous advances, the German armies were spent; counter-attack by the Allies during the summer brought about the collapse of the enemy and incredibly quickly there came the Armistice of 11 November.

Throughout the four years of war the Court of the Stationers' Company had met regularly and it may be set to its members credit that in January 1918 they were still going soberly about their business, presumably confident that peace must come and that, in due course, life would return to some degree of normality. Though in May, under the Mastership of Sir Horace Marshall, it had been decided that the Ladies' Court Dinner should be postponed *sine die*, there had been in January a far more significant move. They had decided that a special Committee should be formed with power to co-opt four members of the Livery, to devise a scheme to increase the revenue and, at the same time, to make the Company of more use to its Liverymen. The outcome will be described later.

Meanwhile it is interesting to be reminded of familiar names on the Court of those days, with Sir George Truscott, Sir Thomas Vesey Strong, Waterlow, Unwin, and Bentley.

Among the serving officers whose names came up for consideration as Renter Warden was Major John Murray, the famous publisher, whose request to be put back for another year was granted while 'preserving his rank in the Livery'. On 14 May a Reception was held in the Hall from 4 o'clock to 5.30 'with tea and music' for overseas officers and friends—almost a pre-1914 touch—and an indication that the Court attempted to do something for the thousands of such men who passed through London during the war.

Another sign of those times was the fact that four apprentices were bound at the June Court and details of payment show: 1st year, No money, 2nd 8s. a week, 3rd 9s. 6d., 4th 10s. 6d., then 12s. 6d. and finally 16s. 6d. (82½p). At another level and indicative of the great difference between the closing months of that war and the next was the payment of a 5 per cent dividend on the English Stock—scarcely prudent, perhaps, but a reminder that the Wood Street and Ludgate Hill rents were being safely paid. In June also, Edward Unwin Sr, he of the immense beard, and one of the original 'Unwin Brothers', printers, proposed and saw carried unanimously the motion that there should be a conference with the Livery for 'the interchange of views, information secured and possible recommendations adopted which might be useful to the Executive Committee of the City Livery Committee'. If it sounds a trifle vague, and it is not easy to trace exactly what became of it, one senses a first move to get the Livery involved in something more than an annual dinner. On a broader front the Industrial Reconstruction Council was granted use of the Hall for a series of weekly lectures over the next few months. That was one of many well-intentioned bodies set up to try to improve the post-war world.

In July 1918 an important figure stepped upon the stage when J. R. Riddell, then Principal of the St Bride's Foundation Printing School, sought permission to hold a public meeting in the Hall to further the cause of technical education. Edward Unwin, who had close links with St Bride's for many years, agreed to act as representative of the Company at the meeting. The Printing School was then permitted to entertain, once a week, servicemen 'allied to us' who were passing through London and who were associated with the printing and stationery trade. How many there were and how they were identified one does not know, but these were some indications of genuine concern for contacts with 'the trades'.

By October came the memorandum of recommendations from the Committee which had been appointed in January 1918. Meetings had been held with the London Master Printers' Association and a potentially exciting prospect had opened out. As Blagden describes in his history, the memorandum stated:

A [new] Society connected with printing, publishing and cognate trades should be formed and the Federation should take a building lease of the garden site; on this, and over the hall and the Court Room, the Federation should build offices for its own use and for the use of other bodies; plans had been prepared and the estimated cost was £25,000. In addition, it should have the use of the Company's premises on Mondays, Wednesdays and Fridays and of the hall twice a year (for exhibitions lasting three weeks) at an annual rent of £1,000. The advantage to the Company would be an increase in the Livery, through the proximity of the offices, and the reversion of a valuable building when the lease fell in.

Though the idea of making the Hall a centre for the printing and other trades had, at once, the approval of the Court, matters of detail arose, such as that all members of the new Society's managing body must be Liverymen and members of the federating societies. The scheme was, however, accepted in principle and referred back to the Committee for opening negotiations, then—unaccountably it now seems—no more is heard of the whole idea. Naturally to those disliking it, in their hearts, there were plenty of relatively minor points on which to fasten their objections. The famous garden (in which, as countless after-dinner speakers have reminded the Livery, the 'heretical books were burned') would have been lost with its exquisite plane tree. That has delighted visitors and generations of Assistants whose eyes may stray out of the windows during a Court meeting, but at what a price in terms of unused assets!

A rental of £1,000 per annum in 1919 must have increased by at least ten if not twenty times today and the resultant transformation of the Company's finances, with its abilities to accomplish so much more, must be left only to the imagination. Similarly the prospect of Stationers' Hall being right at the centre of the work of trade associations could have been most stimulating in itself, but further speculation after more than fifty years is pointless; with the advantage of hindsight it is not difficult to pick on shortcomings in a previous generation.

In the same year other attempts were made to devise ways to keep the Livery in touch with the Court and the General Purposes Committee was instructed to consider revival of the Livery Dinner, the old 'Venison Feast'. Also recommendations were approved that there should be a tea-party for everybody and that, four times a year, a quarter of the Liverymen should be invited to a Court lunch at which there should be discussion on some topic. Somewhat surprisingly, Edward Unwin Sr, then Under Warden, thought this not enough and that another committee should give deeper thought to means for further involvement of the Livery. He was defeated by 7 to 4 votes and nothing more seems to have been done, but it was evidence of new thinking on the Court.

In November 1919 came the really bold move, on the part of J. R. Riddell, when he asked to be allowed to present a case personally to the Court and, at the same time, he called a meeting of Liverymen who elected their own committee. The aim was the wholly laudable one of suggesting how members might take a greater interest in the work of the Company. The Court Orders for that month note merely that Messrs Riddell, G. W. Jones, and R. A. Austen-Leigh 'made a statement and then withdrew . . .', but they were the spearhead in a movement to which future Liverymen were to owe much. Sadly, only one of those early pioneers, Austen-Leigh, survived to become Master—more than thirty years later—when he was no longer able to bring to the office the energy and ability of his prime.

While the Court was still considering the Riddell statement, Sir William Waterlow, later Lord Mayor of London and Master of the Company, wrote, actually on Christmas Eve, suggesting that four members of the Livery, chosen by their fellows, should sit on the Court. This was turned down, but valuable seed had been sown. Early in 1920 it was agreed that there should be a Livery Committee of six to act as a go-between, on which printing, publishing, and papermaking interests should be represented. Three of the members chosen by the Livery, R. A. Austen-Leigh, William Will, and William Penman, were to be future Masters. On St George's Day of that year the Livery Committee met for the first time with the entire approval of the Court. Other members were W. C. Corke, H. D. Singer, S. J. Sandle, G. W. Jones, and J. L. Greaves, with J. R. Riddell as Secretary. Just how the number grew to nine is not known, but it was no bad thing because, inevitably, the Committee was the sort of engagement which must have been 'marginal' to some of its more important members who might not always be free to attend. In the event there seemed always to be a good turn-out for the meetings.

Though no formal terms of reference were set out at the start, they may be summarized as:

(a) To enable Liverymen to meet more frequently; prior to 1920 there had been at most no more than one dinner a year and an occasional church service, plus the Ash Wednesday 'Cakes and Ale' which comparatively few attended.

(b) To allow the Livery to participate, in some measure, in the management of the Company.

(c) To encourage the Company to take a greater interest in 'The Trades' (Blagden wrote of it as having 'retired from the Trade' in the nineteenth century).

R. A. Austen-Leigh was elected Chairman and there is evidence that he was extremely effective; certainly he held the office for seven years. It appears a strange chance that he should have been one of the small number who had to wait so long as fifty-four years before serving as Master. Around forty-five years was the more usual span of time in his generation, and some of us have since 'made it' in less. The Secretary of the Livery Committee was, most appropriately, J. R Riddell, who continued as the mainstay for eleven years, only his untimely death preventing his reaching the Court. For the first few years the Clerk, R. T. Rivington, attended the meetings of the Committee, presumably at the insistence of the Court which did regard them with some suspicion. The custom lapsed, doubtless as Court and Committee learned to live together, and the discussions upon the latter then became, perhaps, less inhibited.

At the first meeting it was straightaway agreed to hold a luncheon in the Hall for the Livery and this took place on 16 June 1920. The American Ambassador was hoped for as Chief Guest, but in his absence Sir William Waterlow made the principal speech—on the work and aims of the Committee. There were 120 people present, including guests, and the charge per head was a well-nigh unbelievable 6s. 6d. (32½p) exclusive of wine; it must, however, be remembered that a typical 'pub' lunch of 'meat and two veg and sweet' was about 7½p then and 17½p would be the price of a three-course lunch in the dining-car of an express train. Thus, in the interests of good attendance, the Committee was quite sensible to press the caterers for a lower price and several different firms were tried over the years, but without much success. Also there were complaints about the standards of service. In those days it was always done by waiters, often elderly, shabby, and ill-paid— who frequently did not hesitate to say pointedly, with open and expectant palm, 'I'm leaving you now, sir' as they served the coffee! (It was a wretched business and something which has changed very much for the better since the Catering Wages Act; the much more general employment of waitresses today seems also to tend towards a higher standard of personal appearance.)

In their effort to keep down costs the Committee went so far as to consider providing the cutlery for the meal, but investigation showed that this would mean an outlay of 25s. (£1.25) 'per cover' and the saving allowed by the caterer would be only a shilling on the price of tickets. As a curious concession, however, the caterers did allow a reduction of a shilling a head for the six 'Press lunches'—free tickets were usually sent to the leading newspapers. These minor domestic matters have an interest today as a reminder of the much more modest scale of such entertainment fifty years ago.

The numbers attending the lunches varied from as few as thirty-nine to 150 or more. As is usual, the most popular and well-known figure attracted the largest number. Sir Johnston Forbes-Robertson, the famous actor, brought in 144 for his 'Recollections of a Stage Life'; Lord Birkenhead, then at the height of his powers as a great Advocate, 122 for a talk on 'Tradition'. The enormously productive Edgar Wallace, of whom it used to be said 'Have you read "the midday Wallace"' spoke inevitably on 'Thrillers'. Among highly topical subjects were 'The British Empire Exhibition' (Wembley 1924) by Sir Laurence Weaver, a famous industrial designer; Sir Banister Fletcher, the great architect, on 'The St Paul's Bridge' (to be a new one over the Thames); 'The London Traffic Problem' (thought already to be very serious; all those slow horse-drawn vehicles delaying cars and buses, no colour-light signals, no one-way streets or roundabouts then); and another far-seeing one was by Major Gladstone Murray, a senior BBC man, on 'Wireless Communication: Present and Future'. Regrettably these stimulating subjects produced audiences of only forty or fifty, though they may well have led to more vigorous discussions than was the case after some famous personality had spoken.

Of greater importance, perhaps, from the standpoint of the Livery were talks by the Clerk, on the history of the Company and its plate; by Bernard Kettle, the City Librarian, on the Company's Almanacks; by Herbert Cox on 'Our Livery Company: Some Proposals'; and, of special interest, 'Seven Years of Peaceful Agitation' by R. A. Austen-Leigh at the time of his retirement from the chair in 1927. 'Tubby' Clayton, the much loved wartime padre and founder of 'Toc H', also Dr W. R. Inge, the famous 'Gloomy Dean' of St Paul's, were other speakers, celebrated in their day, and these names demonstrate that the Livery Committee was unquestionably up-to-date in its ideas and that the members had good contacts. Unfortunately, a small loss was usually made upon these lunches and it had to be made up by a whip-round at the year's end with members putting a pound (or a 'ten bob') note into the funds. One year an anonymous donor most handsomely gave £25—well over £250 today—to cover luncheon deficits. It was to be many years before the Court decided to make an annual grant of £100 towards the Committee's expenses. Before that, however, during the 1940s—upon a hint from the then Secretary, George Riddell—the Court did agree to the provision of a bottle of the Company's sherry with which to encourage those attending the Committee's meetings. To those going through their 'wilderness' years in the Company even this gesture had an effect out of all proportion to its material cost.

The first Ladies' Livery Dinner was held on 23 October 1928 with 146 present, to make the Hall comfortably full, at a cost of 10s. per head (50p) and a profit of over £9 was achieved. At the next meeting there was searching discussion of 'the quality and service of the dinner and the nature of the speeches'. It is intriguing to learn from a minute in the following year that for the next dinner 'It was resolved that a musical programme similar to that of last year . . . should be arranged and that dignity would be given to the function by the exclusion of any humorous items.' Somewhat earlier the Committee had embarked upon a series of dances in the Hall, the first in January 1925, which was a thorough success financially. With 150 present and tickets at 10s., including supper, the profit came out at over £29, and yet another pointer to the low costs of those days is the item £9. 9s. 0d. for the six-piece band. At such a time of high unemployment among the middle classes there were plenty of musical young men eager to play saxophone or drums well into the night for little more than £1 per session. The Hall must have seemed a splendid setting for a dance—including that interesting dip in the floor at the south-west corner demanding an extra close hold on one's partner!

This social programme was no mean achievement. It would have been far from the minds of the Court before the establishment of the Livery Committee, but it must have been a considerable factor in drawing younger members of the Company together and engendering a new sense of pride in the Company, especially when they were able to share some of its beauties with wives and girl-friends. Occasionally luncheons had to be cancelled for lack of support and once, in 1921, because of the 'Industrial Crisis'. A Coal Strike and unrest in other industries resulted in a total of 85 million lost working-days that year and many printers had to go on short time for lack of work; small wonder, therefore, that members of the Committee might feel in no mood for any extra expense.

The Committee had earlier made representations to the Court regretting its intention to discontinue, or at least reduce, the number of Company dinners in the early 1920s. The Committee pressed for two dinners a year, with Liverymen paying for them, and even offered to make all the arrangements for such diners if the Court were unwilling to do so; nothing, however, came of this.

At the same time the Livery Committee asked that it might be represented on the Court, also that a statement of the financial position of the Company should be available to the Livery. The latter was not forthcoming and it remains difficult for the average Liveryman to know details of the finances until such time as he reaches the Court. On the first point, however, real progress was made: in 1922 a Joint Committee was appointed consisting of three members of the Court, Sir William Waterlow, Edward Unwin Sr, and F. S. Miles, plus three Liverymen, R. A. Austen-Leigh, H. D. Singer, and Sir Frederick Bowater, to act as a channel of communication between Court and Livery. Exactly how often they met and the details of their discussions are uncertain, but the exchange of ideas undoubtedly bore fruit—certainly the first two of the

Court members were known to wish to see the Livery being brought more into 'the action'.

At all events, the Committee's labours were justified up to the hilt when, on 13 April 1926, the Court agreed to accept Waterlow's suggestion that it would choose two Liverymen—out of four elected by the Livery—to sit as Assistants for one year and then revert to their former seniority on the Livery List. The arrangement was improved in 1929 to two years' service for the Livery Representative. There are further references to this subject later, but for the present we shall leave it here, save for mentioning that the encouragement of the gesture was slightly spoilt by the insistence of the Court that the new Representatives, Austen-Leigh and J. R. Riddell, should provide their own gowns! Fur-trimmed for all Assistants in those days, they were an expensive item, but under the chairmanship of A. Langley a 'Gown Fund' was organized, raising £32 which covered costs of the two new gowns.

So, with the firm establishment of the Committee no longer did the keen young Liveryman need to feel that there was nothing he could do and that no one was interested in him from the time he had paid his fee and responded to his toast at the Court lunch. By taking the trouble to turn up at the Annual Meeting of the Livery—now Common Hall—he could meet others, show a serious interest in the Company, and thus stand a chance of being invited, in due course, to join the Committee. By degrees he could learn that the Court was not the 'dead hand' on affairs that he might have imagined it to be, and he would discover ways in which he could be of service to the Company.

The work of the Livery Committee over the next fifty years will be a recurring theme in this book. While some might say that it has been primarily concerned with relatively small matters, these all 'add up', and if the founder members could see today how much their successors are able to do within the Company and, in particular, how much improved is the atmosphere, as between Court and Livery, they would indeed feel that their labour—and their courage—was not in vain.

One or two extracts from the court orders (in effect the

Minutes of Court Meetings) of the early 1920s provide a glimpse
of the very different scale in the financial dealings at the time,
even with some allowance for inflation. The main income of
the Company was, of course, the rent from the two small City
properties which amounted to about £4,500; the part-time
services of Reginald T. Rivington (father of Christopher), then
the fourth member of his family to act as the Clerk, were
rewarded very modestly as were those of the Beadle, William
Poulten. The latter also acted as Secretary to the Publishers'
Association and held one or two other minor appointments for
the small organizations, such as the Royal Literary Fund, which
had a room in the Company's building. Mr Rivington, as many
will still recollect, was a striking personality with a magnificent
voice which not even the most elderly Assistants could fail to
hear in Court. Despite lameness due to arthritis, his energy
enabled him to walk a considerable distance daily—between
home and railway station—until he was in his seventies.
William Poulten, too, was a remarkable character, looking with
his high 'stick-up' collar the very image of a Victorian 'beadle'
and until old age, he bathed every morning all the year round
in the Highgate Ponds. As Liveryman No. 351, I recall sitting
next to him at a Civic Dinner and, nourished as I had been in a
teetotal household, was greatly intrigued to see the relish with
which he carefully warmed his brandy, then tipped it into his
coffee. Such was the main staff of the Stationers' Company
fifty years ago, with the aid of a lady wielding a rickety
typewriter. They might be utterly lost in the complexities of
today but, as could be seen in many another organization of
the time, they knew their job and kept the show going with
remarkable economy.

Receipts from the Copyright Registry then were quite
surprising considering that legal register for the United
Kingdom ceased in 1912. At the total of £125 for one year it
suggests about 400 entries at the then rate of fees. Still making
its regular contribution in the 1970s, the Registry continues
also to provide an interesting sidelight on some of the curious
publications of our times.

Other evidence of the extremely small earnings of the Company's staff at that time was the £72 per annum paid to the Hall Keeper, which was, in 1920, put up to £100. Free accommodation would have been included and, doubtless with some of the food also finding its way to him, he would not have done badly bearing in mind that many of the population were then thankful to be earning a steady £3 per week. Yet with this apparently modest way of life it became necessary to sell £500-worth of the Company's Funding Loan Stock in order 'to meet the expenses of the Master and Wardens'.

A serious problem arose in 1928 when death-watch beetle was discovered in the great 12 by 12-inch oak king posts in the roof of the main Hall. They were, of course, out of sight above the ceiling and it was extremely fortunate that the trouble came to light no later. Our present architect, Geoffrey Gurney, working as a junior in the firm of architects then in charge of the Hall, remembers how at the time steel trusses were fitted to take the weight of the roof off the timbers. (This proved providential, under wartime bombing in 1940, when fire at the north end of the Hall destroyed a third of the roof; in the post-war rebuilding all the new trusses were of steel and none of the original oak of the roof remains. Many useful articles, such as gavels for Trade associations, were made from it, the most interesting for us being the stand for our Barge Master's badge, which is itself a model of two of the original oak trusses. This was the gift of Herbert Cox when he was Master in 1943-44.)

Comparison of the *Livery Lists* of that period and those of today is interesting, but one hopes that any future student of the Company's affairs will agree that those of our time are more efficiently done and offer more useful material. The typical *List* of the 1920s runs to no less than 54 pages against the customary 36 or 40 of today, but what one misses so sorely from the old ones is a Master's Report of his year. That excellent practice—however a busy man may regard it at the end of his year of office—was not instituted until the early 1940s. Instead, one finds, year after year, the interminable list of all Past Masters from 'Thomas Dockwray 1556' and this, running for eleven verso pages, was, for some inexplicable reason, printed opposite the names of the Livery, all of which were on recto pages. Details of the same Pension and Scholarship Funds are set out annually, descriptions of banners and pictures on the premises are given, and one is always reminded of the three surviving publications of the Company: the Diary and Year Book, the Almanac, and Carey's *Gradus Ad Parnassum*. More interesting is the list of Prize-winners of the Stationers' Company and Printing Industry Technical Board, a body set up by the Company to encourage technical education. It held craft classes and annual examinations in Stationers' Hall, for which prizes were awarded, including the Company's Silver Medals—some of which may be seen today in the Library. A student of some promise in the year 1927 appears to have been one G. L. Riddell, who walked away with prizes for Composition, Lithography, Cylinder Machine, Stereo and Electro, and Paper. A good comprehensive training was given covering also Costing, Reading, Warehouse, and Book Crafts.

A personal memory of the end of that decade may help to fill in the picture a little for present-day readers. It is of the first Tuesday in July 1929, the day on which your author was 'Cloathed' and, seemingly like all those days on which the new Master first takes the chair, it was hot and sunny. Led into the presence of the Renter Wardens, clutching my cheque—then for only £48—I was most kindly received by Captain Frank Garrett, an able and charming man, whose death in his early years on the Court was a tragedy. One heard the splendid voice of the Clerk boom forth from 'within' and William Poulten seemed continually to sweep in and out of the Court Room at considerable speed. At length my moment came and, not without some trepidation, I entered to make my bow to Master and Wardens.

To a youth of twenty-four the Court appeared even more venerable than one had expected. There were at least four or five white beards among them, and one must remember that any sort of beard was pretty unusual in those days (as witness the existence of that rather absurd 1920s game of 'Beaver'). My family contributed two of them with the Edward Unwins, who incidentally established a record then with father and son simultaneously on the Court for about four years, the Senior surviving until he was nearly ninety-three. Another dear old gentleman, Sir Cecil Harrison, was the retiring Master, who actually received me, before giving way that day to Sir William Waterlow. Other prominent Assistants were Sir George Truscott, Lord Marshall, Lord Ebbisham (Lord Mayor 1926–27), and Alderman Percy Greenaway. There were amongst them men of considerable distinction and achievement, five of 'Lord Mayoral' timber for a start, but the average age of the senior dozen of them could not have been less than seventy-six, of whom four were close on, if not in excess of, ninety! Such men would have been educated and grown up entirely in Victorian days, while much of their working life would have been under the secure conditions of the pre-1914 world when there was little doubt as to the precise positions of master and man—or senior and junior. It was indeed an achievement for such men to have accepted the idea of the Livery Committee. As a gathering they were extremely impressive to a young Liveryman and one hopes that we Assistants of today manage to give as friendly a welcome to the newcomer.

Though my great-uncle Edward had generously provided the wherewithal for my fees, he did not warn me that I should be expected to rise to my feet and respond to a toast at the Court lunch. Perhaps it was just as well because I remember greatly enjoying the meal; the food seemed superb—though I *was* then teetotal. Never shall I forget the horror which came upon me as, after a number of toasts, Sir William Waterlow, an extremely fine figure of a reigning Lord Mayor, rose once more, to deal with the health of 'our new Liveryman especially welcome because he bears a name so well-known to us . . .' Mine was about the briefest response on record which brought more congratulations than it deserved because, I was told, 'you will make a good Master one day if your speeches are always as short as that'—advice which one tried not to forget forty-two years later.

One more recollection of that year is, perhaps, worth recall: the visit of the Prince of Wales to our Civic Dinner of 1929. It was my first Livery Dinner and my experience of 'banquets' had then risen no further than the annual dinner of my School Old Boys' Club. Prior to the rebuilding after the last war the entrance one used to Stationers' Hall was that door under the archway into which the splendid pair of chestnut horses would clatter as they drew in the Lord Mayor's carriage and were thus enabled to get a convenient turn back into the street without the complexities of backing. It is still a good entrance for the Distinguished Visitor who can be received by the Master and led straight up to the Stock Room, but in 1929 the only accommodation for coats was a tiny room like a large cupboard immediately inside that door. There, two attendants worked at high speed to fold and stack some 200 coats and hats on large shelves and there was nowhere at that point to 'brush up'; thereafter one proceeded as at present, to be received in the Stock Room and on to the Court Room. Even the miniscule staff of those days managed somehow to produce the convenient 'personalized' menu and seating plan with the rubber-stamped finger pointing to one's place at table.

My first thrill was to learn that owing to a slight indisposition on the part of my great-uncle Edward (he had by that time consumed about a hundred Livery Dinners), he would not be present and that I was to occupy his seat. Though as a Past Master he was entitled to the top table, he wisely preferred, on account of deafness, to sit at the top of a centre sprig, whence one has that unrivalled view of the most distinguished people present. So, by the merest fluke, I came to dine within no more than ten feet of the Heir to the Throne. One could study at close quarters every movement and gesture and every sartorial detail of the 'best dressed man in England' and sense a little of the enormous charm and vitality which by then was world renowned. In the sad years ahead it was something that one never forgot.

That evening we had for the first time, I believe, the flood-lit windows in operation: the equipment was the imaginative gift of Sir Cecil Harrison and long before the general flood-lighting of the exterior of public buildings, this gave Stationers' Hall a very fine feature. Though I was told that the menus had been much simplified and shortened since earlier days, there were seven courses at least, including that Sorbet to cool us down in the middle (as it used to do for King Edward VII); for a youthful constitution it was all magnificent and in such distinguished company one felt exceedingly proud to be a small part of a great occasion.

CHAPTER TWO

Expansion in the Thirties

I T COULD BE SAID THAT, by comparison with the previous decade the 1930s marked fewer really substantial advances in the powers of the Livery, but it was certainly a period of consolidation in their gains. The regular Livery Luncheons held in the Hall and paid for by Liverymen themselves made an attractive meeting-point. While this may be seen by some as a relatively small matter, it gave the junior members of the Company a real form of participation—'a show of their own'—which they got up for themselves and to which they could have the pleasure of inviting guests.

Unhappily, by 1930 the country was moving into more serious depression and the number of new Liverymen seriously declined. H. A. Cox, later to be Master (1943), was an active member of the Livery Committee. With the aim of revitalizing the Company to make it more attractive to new members he put forward proposals which were aimed mainly at reducing the average age of the Court, giving the Livery a greater share in the actual running of the Company, and earlier opportunity to acquire stock.

Not unnaturally these ideas commended themselves to the Committee which then put forward, from the Annual General Meeting of the Livery on 26 May 1930, what must have seemed to the Court a very drastic programme:

(1) Every Liveryman called into Court should agree to retire one year after serving as Immediate Past Master.
(2) Every third vacancy on the Court should be filled by a

Liveryman taken out of seniority (i.e., without regard to his position in the Livery List).

(3) Widows should not inherit stock.

The principle of item (2) was largely accepted in the very important reorganization of Court Elections in the 1960s except that it provides for an *additional* five Assistants to be elected out of seniority (in effect, every sixth vacancy out of thirty). Item (1) in some form might find its sympathizers even today, but the term of one year only seems unduly harsh; moreover, the situation has been eased by the institution of the Supernumerary List. None of these proposals was adopted then and their rejection seemed to lead to a period when the relations of Court and Livery Committee deteriorated to an unfortunate extent. Nevertheless, some interesting seed had been sown even if the plants were to take several years to mature.

It is convenient here to record the efforts made by the Livery Committee to foster the 'Trades' interest represented in the Company, though some took place in the previous decade. Many would naturally wish to recapture some of the influence formerly held by the Company in the Trade; many would think it a good idea, but the problem was then—and still is—how best to do it.

At the first meeting of the Committee in 1920 W. C. Corke had urged that greater use should be made of the Hall for Trade purposes. He doubtless felt as Blagden was to write forty years later: 'Stationers' Hall stands like a once busy and handsome little port which, through changes in economic conditions and a failure to keep the channels dredged, the tide of commercial life has left high and dry.'

Mr Corke was asked to submit a scheme, but he was evidently—like so many of us—better at stating a problem than at the hard thinking and planning necessary to find a solution: there is no record that any scheme came forth. Later in the same year he again raised the question of 'Linking up the Company with present day needs'. He was once more invited to bring suggestions to the next meeting, but nothing appears to have happened. Early in 1921 *all* members were asked to attend the next meeting with their suggestions, but little resulted. Then a Mr J. L. Greaves was invited to submit a paper at the next meeting in April, but he failed to turn up.

In May of that year it was suggested that a 'Business Club' be formed (oddly enough only £1. 1s. subscription for the Livery, but a quite stinging £10. 10s. for others). Just what they would get for their money and how the minuscule Hall staff would have coped with such an undertaking one cannot imagine, but at the AGM a month later this bold idea became the subject of a resolution that 'the matter lie on the table'. However, all was not stillborn. Representatives were appointed *from the Livery*— which could scarcely have happened before the existence of the Committee—to the Stationers' Company and Printing Industry Technical Board which held its examinations annually in the Hall. The Company agreed to allow the Board to hold a series of Craft Lectures in the Hall and they ran from 1922 until the outbreak of war in 1939. The first lecture was given, in October 1922, by no less a personality than the famous and highly successful Lord Riddell on 'The Printing Business as a Career'— a splendid subject by one of its greatest exponents. These lectures and the examinations did much for the education of printers at all levels in the 1920s and 1930s, and it was a pity that there seemed to be no one to revive them after the war. Thus was an interesting opportunity lost for the Company to do more towards 'getting back into the Trade'.

Arising from one of the Craft Lectures, however, the Company took a prominent part in the formation of the Printing Industry Research Association (PIRA), a body formerly known as PATRA. This achieved a great deal for the introduction of science to printing. In April 1929 Sir Cecil Harrison, the then Master, convened at the Hall a meeting of trade associations and it was out of this that PATRA was actually formed. The Company gave further help by providing free office accommodation at the Hall during the first two years of the Association's life.

Over the years the Livery, through its own Committee and

the Joint Committee with the three Court Assistants, pressed the Court on a variety of subjects, e.g.:

Publication of the Company's Accounts.
Redemption of the English Stock.
Protest on the admission of authors to the Livery.
Unsatisfactory arrangements for admission of distinguished Honorary Freemen (with reference to the previous protest, it is curious to find that Rudyard Kipling and J. M. Barrie were the Freemen concerned).

As the years passed, the Court sometimes reversed former procedure and actually invited the Committee's views *before* taking some action, and, when setting up a House Committee in 1927 to deal with Hall lettings, the Court invited the Committee to appoint three members to it.

During the 1930s the finances of the Livery Committee remained exiguous in the extreme; a credit balance of a few shillings at the end of the year was an achievement. In 1935 its funds sustained a crippling blow when 24 shillings (£1·20) was stolen from the Secretary's office and had to be written off. At another time a member of the Committee, R. Metchim, who did its printing, most generously kept it solvent by allowing a year's credit and then adjusting the amount of its account by its ability to pay! Some faith was required to keep going in such circumstances, and long before it received any grant from the Company.

The Committee did excellent work in encouraging the Court to support the School and the sporting activities of the Old Boys' Association. When the Court showed reluctance to support the Old Stationers Football Club, the Committee sent out a circular to all the Livery, inviting them to become members for a nominal subscription and, in 1936, encouraged their support for the new Pavilion Fund. Later, substantial help was given in the raising of £2,500 (far above £25,000 today) from the Livery for the new playing fields at Winchmore Hill. For that, Lord Iliffe generously contributed no less than £470.

Good work was also done during the Great Depression of the 1930s in exhorting members of the Livery to take boys from the School into their businesses wherever possible; it was then an even more discouraging time for school-leavers. There were 3 million unemployed and the State 'benefit' was minimal.

Somewhat strangely to us, when we now have to limit our numbers, there was anxiety at the decline in the number of the Livery. Ever ready with suggestions, the Committee came forward with the proposal that fines and fees of incoming men should be payable by instalments, and that every fifth vacancy on the Court should be filled from the Livery regardless of seniority; a luncheon club, too, should be set up at the Hall for Liverymen. However, before these bold ideas could be properly considered, Hitler's war had come and any such innovations had to be shelved 'for the duration'.

But, to leave the Livery Committee and to return to other preoccupations of the Court: there was the coming problem of space in the Hall. An absolute maximum of two hundred was the number which could sit down to dinner while still leaving space for a buxom lady singer and her partner to reach the piano. (In less sophisticated times and before we could call upon the Royal Marines Band, such sentimental entertainment had its charms.) Also, when the Company could still afford to entertain us all to dinner without charge, the percentage of acceptances was high; consequently not more than about one-half of the Livery was invited to each dinner.

Of very direct concern both to future numbers in the Livery and to the capacity of the Hall was the matter of the Company of Newspaper Makers—a subject of great importance which must now be dealt with. That Company was an entirely modern creation, being incorporated only in 1931, and it received a Royal Charter in 1933; it had a membership of 162, of whom, as Blagden tells us, 130 were annual subscribers and the rest were honorary or life members. Even before they had secured their Charter, the Newspaper Makers had approached the Stationers with a suggestion for amalgamation. The idea came inevitably as a shock to many members of the Court: the union of an ancient City Company, dating back to 1403, with another a mere two years old, must have seemed incongruous to say the least. There was no lack of critics for the proposal; on the other hand, the mutual advantages were not to be lightly dismissed. The new Company wanted a Hall and a part in the traditions of an ancient corporation; for the Stationers there was the prospect of a substantial number of new members, some of whom were unquestionably rich and distinguished, including, for example, Colonel the Honourable J. J. Astor, then proprietor of *The Times*, Lord Kemsley of the *Sunday Times*, Lord Iliffe, and such brilliant men as Blumenfeld of the *Daily Express* and Simon of the *Daily Telegraph*.

Besides them there were also several lively minds who could help to strengthen our ties with Fleet Street and with the world of what was becoming known as Public Relations. Among them was a future Master, Cuthbert Graseman, Publicity Manager of the Southern Railway. It involved also the startling innovation of ladies to the Livery. Others of the prospective newcomers were H. A. Gwynne of the *Morning Post*, Robert Lynd of the *News Chronicle*, John Gordon and Charles de Ryck of the *Sunday Express* (and later of the *News Chronicle*), Sir Robert Evans of *Education*, Commander Kenworthy (later Lord Strabolgi), and John Betts of the *City Press* and Roy Pratt-Boorman of the *Kent Messenger*, both of whom served upon the Court. After considerable discussion, including consultation with the Livery, the vote, as we all know, went in favour of the amalgamation, and on 22 May 1933, the Court approved the steps by which complete integration was to be achieved. On 16 October of that year Renter Wardens worked as never before with the admission of eighty-seven Newspaper Makers; it would be interesting to know just how they were dealt with in the Court Room and whether they all made the Declaration as 'one man' or in groups. All were properly welcomed at lunch afterwards and, presumably, toasts were proposed *en masse* and the senior Newspaperman would have replied on behalf of all of them.

The new Liverymen of the Stationers' Company took their

place at the end of the existing list which suddenly jumped to well over 400 and five of them were made Assistants, thus increasing the size of the Court to thirty for a few years to come. It was also understood that R. D. Blumenfeld, who had been admitted a week earlier, should be added to the Court on his return to the country from a long visit overseas. A very fine after-dinner speaker, he it was who coined the phrase 'the worshipful company of Harrisons'—at a time when that great name accounted for eleven entries in Court and Livery Lists.

Three more of the newcomers were promised places on the Court in 1939, 1945, and 1951—the individuals unspecified—and several of our own senior Liverymen must have resented this additional hindrance to their own progress towards the Court. Though all the new men paid up the normal fees as for Livery and Court, thus netting the Company a welcome extra £4,000 and more in 1933, there was 'murmuring' among some that the Newspapermen had been admitted too cheaply. It is difficult to judge at this date, but unquestionably the Company has gained much over the years. Whether our predecessors envisaged the number of revolutionary forms of communication to be developed in the next half-century is another matter, but it is certain that it would have been a tragedy if two Livery Companies, each concerned for preservation and freedom of the printed word, had not combined their resources.

Besides the entry of the Newspapermen, the year 1933 was remarkable in other ways; though admirably described by Blagden, they are summarized here because they bear directly upon events in the next part of our story. Sir Percy Greenaway, father of Sir Derek and Alan, a 'Pickwickian' figure, of unfailing courtesy even to a Renter Warden, was both Master and Lord Mayor of London in May 1933. He was re-elected with his Wardens in July on the understanding that, after six months, he would make way for R. D. Blumenfeld on his return to England. On 5 December, however, Sir Percy announced that the Prince of Wales had agreed to accept the honorary Freedom and Livery of the Company *and to serve as Master*.

A Special Court was held early in the evening of 20 December, at York House, St James's, for the installation of His Royal Highness and one cannot help observing that twenty-four Assistants were present, whereas at the first October Court there had been only eleven. The Civic Dinner followed, the same evening, with the Prince presiding over a record attendance. He had previously shaken hands with each one of us as we entered the Hall and, after initial surprise at his extreme shortness, one remained deeply impressed not only by the galaxy of his decorations but by the concentrated, penetrating gaze of the very blue eyes—that royal touch which enables the subject to feel that for a few seconds *he* is the one who matters! So great was the number present that about fifty of the more junior Liverymen had to take their dinner in the Court Room—a considerable disappointment for many (and one, at least, was shocked to find that the Baron of Beef was, intentionally, served cold). However, we were admitted to the Hall for the speeches and some of us stood against the wall behind the top table. One still recollects the consummate skill with which our Royal Master delivered his amusing and informal-sounding speech. He read it from notes set on top of a forest of long-stemmed hock glasses, but turned his head easily from left to right in order to throw his voice to the ends of the Hall, glancing imperceptibly at his text on each turn to pick up the following phrase. The Livery Committee had not then, it should be noted, given that exceedingly useful small oak reading-desk to the Company. Naturally the Prince could not be expected to fulfill the normal duties of Master of our Company and Sir Percy Greenaway continued as Deputy Master until Blumenfeld took over in November 1934.

As a result of these interesting 'irregularities'—approved of course by the Court at the time—coupled with the build-up of potential Masters on account of the enlarged Court, it was arranged that for the next five years Masters should serve for only six months each. Some of them may have welcomed the shorter term, but in the main one feels that they were unfortunate. It takes the average man, even after some years on the Court, at least two or three months before he begins to be at home as Master, with all that it entails, and to be 'out' just as he is starting to enjoy it all must have seemed frustrating, to say the least. However, the plan certainly provided opportunity for somewhat earlier advancement for many of us in later years.

The enlarged Livery, which could no longer be accommodated at one sitting, gave rise to the idea of the extension of the Hall. Plans were prepared and a handsome brochure printed with architect's drawings reproduced in it. The new section would have come across the courtyard to the east, forming a T-section with the main Hall. The top table would presumably have run along the west wall, below the stained-glass windows, and diners in the new extension would have been able to see only a part of the more distinguished company. It would have cost £60,000 and one is surprised to learn that the plan was approved in 1935, when the economy was beginning, only slowly, to recover from the severe depression which certainly affected both the printing and publishing trades. On the other hand, there were then some quite wealthy members of the Company and though (with recollection of pre-1914 days) they might well complain of the rate of taxation, it did still leave a rich man free to dispose of much more of his money as *he* wished. In fact, the Prince's relinquishment of Mastership early in 1936 suggested that future acceptances of dinner invitations were unlikely to be so heavy and, of course, the cost to the Company of giving everyone a free dinner twice a year—had that been the intention—would have been a serious extra expenditure. Altogether, and especially in view of the economic problems of the 1970s, it was fortunate that no such extension was ever built. One can imagine the outcry today if even an ancient City Company tried to tamper in such a manner with its own Building of Historic Interest.

While the Company was not notable for pronouncements upon the problems of the Trades of the Guild, the Court lifted up its voice in 1935 to protest to the Prime Minister, Stanley Baldwin, then an Honorary Freeman and Liveryman. The objection was to the growing number of publications produced by the Government 'which in the opinion of the Court should properly be entrusted to private firms'. The Publishers' Association might well have been behind this, but the matter was undoubtedly of concern also to printers; it was and continues to be a form of State-subsidized competition on a scale which few other industries suffer to the same extent. The effect of that protest, and many others since—alas—can be gauged from the enormous present-day output of Her Majesty's Stationery Office as displayed in the Government Bookshops. Thanks to that move in 1935 the authorities can at least be in no doubt as to views of those whose livelihood depends upon the printed word.

By the year 1937 the Government's rearmament programme was beginning to have some effect in stimulating the economy and many businesses were becoming a little more profitable; it seems strange that in 1938 when the same trend was continuing, the Court appeared to be still determined upon economies. One Livery dinner was cut altogether and the Court ruled that for the future no dinner invitations should be sent to those who did not pay their fine for not serving as Renter Warden. It now seems a modest enough sum, but to a young Liveryman in pre-war days it could loom as quite an item, likely to hit one at an awkward moment in early married life (in my own case, at the time of the Fall of France in 1940 and the birth of a second child, and long before the Welfare State!).

To return to the economy drive, in a self-denying ordinance the Court also decided to reduce its own fees, five guineas (£5·25), by half and, curiously, ordained that the Ladies' Dinner should 'stand over'. If it seems unduly parsimonious to us, with our much greater financial problems, it must be remembered that the Company's income was then very small, dependent almost entirely upon the rents from the Ludgate Hill and Wood Street properties, with, of course, that from Simpkin Marshall, the great book wholesalers in Stationers' Hall Court. What one has also to remember is that the Hall, with its poorly equipped cloakrooms, was not then so readily 'lettable' and the scale of fees for its use was inevitably low, so that little income could be obtained from that source. It is not really surprising, then, that as prices began to rise, some alarm was felt.

That fateful year of 1939 was the last in which the plan of Masters serving only six months each was in operation. During the previous four years holders of such famous names—in Company annals—as Adlard, Baddeley, Truscott, Clay, Waterlow, and Austen-Leigh, each of whom would surely have made excellent full-time Masters, were passed quickly through the Chair. E. C. Austen-Leigh and Edward Unwin Jr (son of the more venerable one we met in the previous chapter) were the Masters for 1939 and there is little record of any preparations being made for war during that summer. One finds no mention of emergency plans for the removal of the Company's treasures to some safer spot outside London. Indeed, until several more years had passed our priceless records, many of them dating back to the sixteenth century, were not kept in reliably fireproof conditions. These problems were not seriously faced until the bombs began to fall in 1940.

Meanwhile it was definitely decided that plans for the extension to the Hall should stand over. The principal tenants, the Publishers' Association and the Booksellers' Association, continued to occupy their small offices in the basement, holding their respective Council Meetings in the Court Room. It is striking evidence of the enormous growth of Trade associations, over the past thirty years, when one considers the large buildings now required to house each of these organizations in the 1970s.

Few, if any, of those who enjoyed the Spring Livery Dinner at Stationers' Hall on a May evening in 1939 could have conceived that nearly twenty years were to pass before they were again to have the pleasure of dining at their Hall in 'Evening Dress with Decorations'. During the long years of war, austerity, and an unusable Hall, many must have wondered whether those times would ever come again. Yet for some Liverymen, even in war, there was at least the occasional Court lunch, maybe as Renter Warden or on joining the Stock Board, when the sight of the panelled walls and the old shields, above the aroma of good port and cigars, could serve as a reminder of former pleasures and give a gleam of hope for the future. Beside the many other functions of the Stationers' Company it must be freely admitted that to meet, to dine, and to entertain guests in the Hall must remain one of the major satisfactions of any Liveryman, however conscientiously he may take his part in other activities.

Shortly after the outbreak of war in September 1939 units of the 2nd Battalion the London Rifle Brigade were billeted in the Hall, perhaps its one claim to war service, and one would like to think that they were more comfortable than in many of the strange buildings suddenly commandeered then. They did not stay long and after a lunch for Court and Livery in December, the one major engagement for Edward Unwin's six months Mastership, there was no further entertaining in the Hall as England moved into the years of her total war effort.

CHAPTER THREE

The Second World War

WAR LEFT STATIONERS' HALL comparatively
undisturbed until the night of 15 October 1940, when the
roof was destroyed by incendiary bombs. But for the courage-
ous action of our Hall Keeper, Mr Price, we should almost
certainly have lost the entire building. Singlehanded, at first, he
dashed up to the roof and dealt with the fire bombs, using the
famous long-handled shovel then provided for the purpose. His
prompt action was especially brave for a man not of the
strongest physique and no longer young. In the event, the roof
with its exquisite ceiling was almost entirely destroyed; a rough
temporary structure kept out the rain but not the wind and
general damp, so that the Hall was entirely unusable and
desolate for the rest of the war and some years after. The Court
Room was also damaged beyond repair, its south wall pushed
dangerously out of the perpendicular.

For the next fifteen years the Court held its meetings in the
Stock Room, which remained the only part of the premises
usable for a gathering of any kind. For the actual meeting
Assistants sat in the customary horseshoe formation and at the
end, Mr Price and his staff quickly moved tables out from the
wall, laid the lunch, and rearranged all the chairs. By the time
members had picked their way down the unheated and
draughty Hall for a wash in the spartan accommodation, then at
the south end, and returned to the Stock Room, there was an
excellent lunch awaiting them—the wine cellar having
remained intact. A Renter Warden's memory of those days
included the superlatively high quality of Price's coffee,
unequalled by any of his successors. When asked where it came

from, he replied that it was 'Lyons', but the secret lay in the method of making: an old porcelain drip percolator (which appears long since to have vanished). Price was a wonderful servant of the Company, maintaining standards under great difficulties.

After this disaster the Court at once took steps to get the Company's treasures away to a safer spot. Lest it be thought that the Court had been negligent up to then, it should be remembered that a great many responsible people did not believe that London would be seriously bombed and the period of the 'phoney' war up to the summer of 1940 had sustained this view. Twenty years before soaring rents were to drive many businesses out of the City the idea of transferring plant, stocks, and staff into the country was unthinkable. Certainly the majority of publishers in 1939 fully agreed with a defiant advertisement of one great publishing house which read as follows:

> Macmillan & Company, Ltd. in response to numerous enquiries from authors, booksellers and members of the public, wish to state emphatically that they propose to carry on their business at St. Martin's Lane, London, W.C.2., until they are either taxed, insured, A.R.P'd., or bombed out of existence.
> (A.R.P. stood for Air Raid Precautions, the regulations for which were very burdensome for many.)

Despite spectacular losses suffered by some firms, the vast majority of publishers and booksellers at first carried on in London, as did most printers, but some twenty publishers lost their entire premises and much of their stock in the total destruction of the old Paternoster Row.

Sir George Wilkinson who was Lord Mayor during 1940-41, throughout the crucial winter of the so-called Blitz on London, and Master of the Company during 1941-42, was requested by the Court to make a short report at the end of his year in order to keep members well informed of the activities of the Com-

pany under the wholly exceptional conditions. Thus began the
practice—of great interest for our records—and of extreme
value to the historian. Sir George was able to state that the
irreplaceable furniture and fittings of the Hall, especially the
famous Stephen Colledge carved oak screen, and the carving
surrounding the Court Room fireplace, as well as many of the
pictures, Chippendale chairs, etc., had been removed 'to a place
of safety', then unspecified, as a matter of wartime secrecy. In
fact much of it went to the strong-room under Cunard House,
Lower Regent Street, and to the Public Record Office, while
Lady David kindly accommodated the screen at her house in
Henley.

The last major wartime disaster for the Stationers was the
total destruction by fire and high-explosive bombs in December
1940 of the buildings between the Hall and Ave Maria Lane.
These included the tall Victorian block of Simpkin Marshall
who until then had given a service of incalculable value to
booksellers, enabling them to obtain, from that one source, the
books of any publisher. Thereby booksellers had been spared
the labour and expense of having to approach scores of individual publishers for their small orders, often for single copies,
and the latter had been relieved of the enormous amount of
detail involved in the handling of such orders.

More on this subject would be a digression from our main
story, but it is proper that tribute should be paid here to one of
the most important of the Company's former tenants, a firm
which had provided a vital service to the book world and for
whom 'Stationers' Hall Court' had seemed always a wholly
appropriate address.

In the course of his report Sir George Wilkinson was able to
record the more cheerful fact that three new Liverymen had
joined during 1941–42, whereas not a single one had come
forward in the previous twelve months; this may be seen as
significant of the changed attitude in people at the period. From
summer 1940 for nearly a year, on the home front one lived
from day to day, thankful for mere survival, with little idea of
planning far ahead. By the time the bombs on London had

ceased and Hitler had attacked Russia, a great load of the most intense anxiety had been lifted for many. Allied to this was the Livery's concern for those young men in the Forces who were known to want to join the Company but were losing status because they could not make the Declaration of a Freeman. Nor did their present financial position enable them to find the money to pay their fees. When its attention was drawn to the problem the Court resolved unanimously:

1. That, in order to meet the War Emergency conditions, members of His Majesty's Forces who shall apply to the Court for admission to the Livery shall be entered on an Emergency List, showing the date of acceptance of the application in each case.
2. That those on such Emergency List subsequently admitted to the Livery shall take their places in the Livery List according to the date of acceptance in each case.
3. That the making of the Declaration and the payment of the Fee may be postponed for a period terminating six months from the date of demobilisation, or for an extended period at the discretion of the Court.

It was a well thought-out move, nicely calculated to encourage those who might otherwise have lost up to six years in their seniority and decided that it was not worth their while to enter the Livery at all.

Sir George, who won great admiration for his dauntless courage as Lord Mayor throughout the worst of the London raids, concluded his report with that ringing verse from Kipling:

> There is but one task for all,
> For each one life to give.
> Who stands if freedom fall?
> Who dies if England live?

adding the hope that we might 'all unite and strive together and never cease in our endeavours until this City rises once again in all its glory, worthy of its great traditions'. Most happily that great citizen and Stationer lived on to see most of his hopes fulfilled.

Earlier in the war, on 5 July 1940, Stationers' Hall was the scene of what became recognized as an historic meeting of distinguished people gathered by Geoffrey Faber, then President of the Publishers' Association, and Stanley Unwin, in protest against the inclusion of books in the proposed purchase tax. Sir Hugh Walpole, the Archbishop of Canterbury, J. B. Priestley, A. P. Herbert, and Dr J. J. Mallon were a few of the large audience who crowded in, concerned that, even in the midst of world war, books should not be classed among those things of which the distribution and sale should be artificially discouraged. That protest meeting turned the tide of opinion and within a few weeks the Chancellor, Sir Kingsley Wood, announced in Parliament that, contrary to his previous assertion, books *would* be exempted from purchase tax. The wartime benefit to the reading public—to say nothing of the printers and publishers of books—was beyond reckoning.

After 1940 the reign of the Master reverted to the normal span of twelve months and Herbert A. Cox as a Chartered Accountant had some interesting figures to present in his report for 1943–44. His father and grandfather had each occupied the Chair before him and his ownership of the technical journal *The Builder* qualified him further for the Livery. (He was a man of original mind and many may still recall his curious habit of wearing a black silk skull cap when in Court, which lent a very strange air of distinction to the gathering.) He pointed out that the one man called on to Court during his period of office, E. Russell Polden, had received his call within only twenty-six years, whereas the two senior members of his own Court had each had to wait for forty-six years. These were remarkable extremes; save for certain of the senior Newspapermen, or the occasional Alderman, the normal period for ascent to the Court solely on seniority is about thirty-five years. It is probable that a sudden succession of deaths ahead of him had been responsible for Mr Polden's rapid progress.

This vexed matter of Court selection will be discussed later: obvious as are the disadvantages of unduly old men in that position, there are also sharp limits to the number of middle-aged Liverymen, probably at the height of their careers and with heavy demands upon their time, who can free themselves to devote parts perhaps of several days a month to the affairs of the Company. 'Time-off' may be taken less easily by the employed director or manager of a public company than was the case by his father, for instance, who might have been the principal shareholder in a smaller concern.

The death of William Poulten, noted in that same report, severed a link which stretched back into Victorian times, and his faithful service as the Company's Beadle for fifty years was properly recorded. Until he was succeeded by Ernest Mettrop, just before the war, Poulten—at certain levels and to many people—*was* Stationers' Hall. If you wanted anything to do with the Company, he steered you to it, including the Registry; the then little Publishers' Association employed him as Secretary, likewise the Royal Literary Fund, and he kept an eye on the Associated Booksellers, who met at the Hall monthly. These others had their diminutive offices in the block of the Stock Room, mainly in the basement.

In contrast to the present, Mr Cox was able to note that no fewer than sixteen apprentices had been bound during his year, whereas today so large a number is unknown. It is understandable that, with the decline in the number of London printers, there should be many fewer apprentices brought to us, but the virtual cessation of the practice is regrettable. Ten years ago it was the exception to hear the Clerk announce: 'There are no apprentices today, Master.' Then there could be as many as four at a time standing beside their fathers, frequently with mothers in attendance at the back of the Court Room. It was a ceremony perhaps archaic, but of undoubted charm and one which could not fail to impress many youngsters and their parents. Most Masters of the Company prepared their 'Addresses' to apprentices with considerable care (and one, at least, was sad to need his only once in 1971–72). No one who served on the Court under the Mastership of John Mylne ('Jack') Rivington can ever forget the inspiring mixture of wisdom, humour, and encouragement which he imparted so easily and informally to apprentices in his time.

It should be mentioned that all through the war the Livery Committee continued to meet regularly in the Stock Room, maintaining its interest in the hoped-for reforms and preparing its Annual General Meeting, when names for the new Livery Representative and Renter Wardens would be put forward. Although against the background of mighty international events their activities were trivial in the extreme, it was no bad thing to carry on 'business as usual' where possible: so many activities in all walks of life were then suspended, never to be revived.

The imperturbability of the ordinary citizen does come through even in the Committee Minutes of those times. At the meeting of 15 May 1941, it was reported that 'the Minutes could not be read because the Minute Book could not be salvaged from the premises of the Hon. Sec. which had been damaged by enemy action'. In fact those premises had been completely destroyed by the last great manned-bomber air raid on London, that of 10 May 1941. Yet at the height of the Blitz, there was the Committee soberly meeting to elect its Representatives and the School Governors, and pressing the Court to hold another service in St Paul's to replace the cancelled Ash Wednesday one, and so on.

Directly the future became brighter, with the huge American army and air force building up here, the Committee returned to its reforming programme and in the summer of 1944, just as the dreaded V1 and V2 pilotless planes were doing great damage for a short time. That was when the then Master, Herbert Cox, gave his valuable talk on 'Post-War Problems of the Company' and the Committee made the first of various representations on membership of the Court and wider distribution of the English Stock, and pressed for rapid rebuilding of the Hall.

Already the financial problems of the Company in war

conditions were causing much anxiety as the English Stock, dependent mainly upon rents, had virtually no income. Though expenses were cut to a minimum, even the costs of simple Court lunches and the salaries of the tiny staff had to come mainly out of capital. However, as the war drew towards its end, a determined drive for more Liverymen was made. This took the form of a persuasive letter to a number of publishers by Charles J. Watts, Master 1944-45, in which he pointed out the part which revived Livery Companies should be able to play in the post-war world. It was well timed because, as Watts was doubtless aware, publishers were prosperous then and were having to pay out large sums in Excess Profits Tax. To divert a very small part of their profit towards entry into the Stationers' Company was an attractive idea to many.

During 1944-45 eight new members were admitted to the Livery and eighteen took up the Freedom, an encouraging sign for the future. These hopes were amply fulfilled in the following year, with no fewer than twenty-seven new Liverymen and thirty-four more Freemen. While it was to be more than ten years before Company activities were to be restored on any scale, these new admissions must have come as a considerable encouragement to those on both Court and Livery Committee who met regularly to discuss and plan for the future while the present was still full of frustration and inaction.

A most stirring and invigorating function in 1946 under the Mastership of Robert K. Burt was the admission to the Honorary Freedom and Livery of Lt-General Sir Bernard Freyberg, VC. By permission of the Lord Mayor the Special Court was held at the Mansion House, our own Court Room being still in ruins, and the ceremony was followed by (what seemed at that time of rationing) a fine lunch in the Egyptian Hall to which the entire Livery was invited. It was an honour for the Company to have that great soldier among us and those present at the time may still recall the magnificent figure he presented—the bronzed face of the New Zealander above the row upon row of medal ribbons. It was also memorable for the Livery—at a domestic level—as the first time they had for nearly seven years been able to meet and enjoy a meal together. Though an isolated occasion, it was one of happy reunion for many and a reminder of one feature of membership which the Company could offer in the years to come. One is interested to observe, incidentally, that in that year Renter Wardenship was in the exceptionally capable hands of 'Mr Denis Truscott and Mr Derek Greenaway', but an apologetic note crept into the report when it referred to revival of the ancient Ash Wednesday custom of distributing 'cakes and ale': 'It is regretted that, owing to prevailing conditions, the buns were not up to the usual standard.'

Though we have now advanced one year beyond the end of the war, that comment on poor quality can stand as the conclusion to this chapter; it was to be a decade and more before the Company was free of the shortages and poor-quality substitutes which made up the years of 'austerity', but each Master was able to record some advance towards the former— and then to much higher—standards of achievement.

CHAPTER FOUR

Reconstruction and Resurgence

AMONG THE DOMESTIC events of the year 1948 was
one of especial pleasure and significance to one section
of the Company—the Livery Committee Luncheon. Held in
the Stock Room, it was paid for by the members themselves.
Some of the food—in those days still of rationing—was
ingeniously obtained by a member with special 'connections' in
an important City market—Billingsgate. Mr Price achieved his
usual high standards and those present felt it was almost like old
times. Described as 'a most enjoyable function' by the Master,
Victor B. Harrison, it also gave Committee members each the
opportunity to invite a guest, and there were but two speeches.
This was the pattern for such lunches, which became annual
affairs, and incidentally provided opportunity for successive
Chairmen to get in a little practice at speaking to Stationers on
a small scale before their time might come to face the much
larger after-dinner audience in the Hall. While it may not seem
an event of great importance, the success of that lunch was a
tonic to those who organized it, as an efficient and friendly
occasion, offering remarkably good value for money and
holding out promise of what the Livery might be able to do for
itself in years to come. It was a generous and encouraging
gesture later for them to be granted the splendours of the
Court Room for the Committee Lunch after the rebuilding had
been completed.

Victor Harrison had the imaginative idea of presenting—to
mark his year of office—the beautiful model of the State Barge
of 1820 owned by the Company. In its glass case it remains on
view to any visitor to the Hall and serves as a reminder of the

fine workmanship and colouring which went into such vessels, as well as recalling something of the magnificence of a Lord Mayor's Show when it used to take place on the Thames in the last century.

At the same time we greatly benefited by the action of a bibliophile Liveryman, Ellic Howe, who among many other activities was writing a centenary history of *The London Society of Compositors*. He sought permission to study the Company records and was so shocked at the haphazard conditions in which they were stored that he offered to donate all his royalties on the book to the Company if we would use the money to reconstruct the old strong-room into a proper fire-proof Muniment Room. His earnings upon the book amounted to over £400, enabling a small room to be created, actually in the form of a large safe, built into one of the walls just beyond the south end of the Hall. It is properly equipped with ample shelving and fire-proof drawers and has adequate space for work at a desk. The idea was a generous one, from which countless scholars and research students have benefited over the past thirty years.

By chance the next Master, for 1948–49, was also a distinguished member of the Harrison family, Guy, who was knighted a few years later, primarily for his valuable wartime work as Chairman of the Joint Industrial Council of the Printing and Allied Trades, which had settled many an industrial dispute. An excellent point he always made in his Address to Apprentices was to tell them that if in the future they became involved in disputes with their employers, they should strive always to remember that there were two sides to every question and that *all* justice did not normally rest on one side: the other fellow deserved consideration too. He was a man of unusual charm and ability and it was regrettable that in his year the Company was still much hampered by its extreme shortage of income.

The first post-war dinner for the Livery, with their wives, was achieved in the Egyptian Hall at the Mansion House on a beautiful evening in May when many must, for the first time, have known the full dignity of that impressive entry of the Lord Mayor and Sheriffs to the traditional accompaniment of the March from Handel's *Scipio*. A total of 260 made a record attendance and the occasion was made the more magnificent by the presence, for the first time, of the band of the Royal Marines. Through Colonel Sir Oliver Crosthwaite-Eyre, later on a Court Assistant, contacts were made which resulted in the proposal at a Court meeting that we should 'adopt' that famous corps, in the same manner as had been done by some City Livery Companies with other regiments.

Since the date of their formation the Marines had always had exceptionally close connections with the City of London and to many on the Court in 1949 the idea was immediately attractive, one of those present emphasizing especially the likelihood that in future one of the Marine bands might well find its way to the Hall to grace our more important occasions. So it came about, and now for very many years a smartly turned-out band, in dress uniform, has played in the Musicians' Gallery of the Hall at our Livery Dinners, and the attendance of the Commandant General of the Royal Marines, with two or three of his officers, has become a splendid part of our tradition. Most years the Hall is lent for some Marine function and fortunate is the Master who is invited to partake of their wonderful hospitality there, or on their home ground at one of their Depots!

By 1950, five years after the end of the war, though much of the City still lay in ruins, albeit with pleasant flower gardens flourishing on many of the vacant plots—as in Warwick Lane— life was returning to the Company in many ways and the fullest use was made of the one part of the premises which was 'operational', namely the Stock Room. Because so many of the other Livery Company Halls had been destroyed by bombing and were not yet rebuilt, there was additional pressure upon any room with some tradition behind it which could accommodate up to, say, a hundred people. Fortunately, during the year when the Muniment Room was finally ready, the Master was Sidney Hodgson, FSA, then head of the famous Chancery Lane firm of antiquarian book auctioneers, now part of

Sotheby Parke Bernet & Co. Mr Hodgson, whose son Wilfrid is now a Warden, had unrivalled knowledge of the Company's records; he had played a large part in the planning of the new Room and it was most appropriate that he should have presided over its formal opening by Sir Hilary Jenkinson, Deputy Keeper of the Records. The occasion was also attended by representatives of the British Museum and the Guildhall Library.

Mr Hodgson, who later became our Honorary Archivist, explained then that the Muniment Room henceforth would house, in greater safety, the Exemplification of our Charter, our Court Books, and Registers, all of which are of inestimable value to research workers, scholars, and students both here and in the United States. Other valuable material was at the same time arranged in a more accessible form. The value of this was soon apparent, as requests were received from the National Register of Archives and also from the Library of the University of Illinois for permission to make copies of certain documents. In that year also, permission was given for an American reprint by photo-litho of the great Arber Transcript of our Registers (of entries at Stationers' Hall) for the years 1554–1650, comprising five large quarto volumes. Though much of this might be out of the sight and knowledge of many Liverymen, it represented one of the great justifications for the existence of the Stationers' Company in the twentieth century.

Other gatherings held in the Stock Room at the time were the Annual Meeting of the British Records Association and the first meeting of the Standing Conference for Local History. The Society of Editors had a social evening with their Ladies present and the Friends of the National Libraries came one afternoon. On each occasion Sidney Hodgson was able to arrange small exhibitions of our Court Books, Registers, and Plate, all of which aroused the keenest interest, especially when the famous Stationers' Almanacs for 1752 were put on show, the year of the Calendar Reform, when eleven days were omitted from the month of September in order to bring Britain into line with the rest of Europe. The success of these small displays was such as to implant the idea of something larger for the year of the 1951 Exhibition.

Another man with exceptional knowledge of various antiquities, who joined the Court at this time, was Robert Wiley Lloyd, who was Chairman of Christies and of a printing company. He had two flats in Albany, in one of which he lived; the other was entirely given over to displays of his superb collection of Turner watercolours, now in the British Museum; 3,800 out of the known 4,000 species of beetles, and Japanese Swords and Chinese lacquer, were also his specialities. He left £1000 to the Stationers' Company, which, though subject to Estate Duty, provided the elegant silver gilt goblets used always by the Master, Wardens, and Treasurer; they are a pleasant memory of a remarkable and generous man.

An historically interesting succession to the Master's chair for 1950–51 was that of the Clerk, Reginald Thurston Rivington, actually the ninth member of his family to hold the office. No other family had provided so many Masters though, as Mr Rivington observed in his Report, 'the Harrison Family are doing their best to catch up'. The great achievement during that year was completion of the restoration of the Hall. Much progress had been made during 1949–50, but the full cost of renewing the beautiful ceiling, it was realized, would not be covered by the settlement of our War Risks Insurance claim. At the time few, if any, Liverymen would have known that the ceiling was all painted on canvas.

An appeal was launched to all members of the Company and the response was most encouraging: one member of the Court gave £250, donations of £100 each came in from four different printing companies, and in a short time the fund was approaching the £3,000 required (it seems little enough today). All the work of the Hall restoration, in its very considerable and intricate detail, was carried out under the direction of Mr Geoffrey Gurney, who has been the Company's architect for many years. He recalls that early in 1941, soon after the bombing of the Hall, the painted canvas was carefully removed from the ceiling, rolled up, and stored for nearly ten years. Though badly damaged by fire and water, there was enough remaining of the design to enable it to be reproduced, after more than 140 years. This was achieved by a young artist, believed to be a pupil of Henry Moore, who, with the original canvas before him, did the work most skilfully in his own studio. When completed, the new canvas was affixed to the ceiling, in strips, while scaffolding was in place for the craftsmen doing the other painting and gilding. The final result was a triumph and no one who had contributed to the cost could have failed to consider that his money was well spent when he saw the restored Hall in its full glory—at night—with the renewed ceiling softly glowing above the diffused lighting.

While, however, Mr Rivington could proudly report on the state of the Hall, it was unfortunately still not possible to use it for any evening function because the heating plant was in the basement below the Court Room and the severity of damage to that 250-year-old building was such that complete reconstruction was essential. Although the shell remained, the roof was in a very bad state and the main wall, facing the garden, had been pushed seriously out of the perpendicular. At least no rates or taxes had to be paid upon the Hall while no form of income could be obtained from it. No building work could be done then without Government licence and another four years passed before the Court Room could be fully restored.

Reginald Rivington was still Clerk to the Company in 1950 and during the year of his Mastership his cousin, Charles Rivington (Master in 1968), undertook part of the Clerk's duties, including, naturally, attendance upon the meetings of the Court and of the Master and Wardens.

A handsome move by the Master was his personal entertainment of the Livery Committee at Luncheon in the Stock Room in November 1950, at which, incidentally, he achieved the feat of rounding up a sufficient number of the attractive little old metal matchboxes, bearing the crest of the Company, to give one to each member present. They had been a regular 'handout' at Livery Dinners in pre-war days, but had long since disappeared. Those who looked back to the early years of attempts to establish some organization for the Livery—when the Clerk had sometimes to convey unwelcome tidings from the Court and when, frankly, the idea of the Committee must have been a distinct nuisance to him!—those older ones must have seen Mr Rivington's luncheon invitation as a very charming gesture. After more than twenty years one can feel that the wish he expressed then, that to help the work of the Committee it would be 'fitting' if more would turn up to the Annual Meeting of the Livery, has been fulfilled.

In September 1951, during the Mastership of Arthur Fowler, the first Dinner was held in the Hall since 1939. Without heating it could be no later in the year and without kitchens a 'special service' had to be arranged, with Ring and Brymer exercising all their ingenuity in odd corners of the premises. Thus the full numbers could not be accommodated, but the Company's wine-cellars had remained intact. Distinguished guests included the Acting Lord Mayor, Sir Frank Newson-Smith and the Archbishop of Canterbury, and the evening proved a great success. It was an undoubted landmark, though no further dinner could be held in the Hall until 1957, when the rebuilding of the Court Room and the Cloak Rooms had been completed. This last item was of great importance for the future letting of the Hall, which was rightly seen as a potential asset of the greatest value. Hitherto, as mentioned earlier, the lavatories for men had been primitive and inconvenient, and there had been no accommodation for ladies, apart from the very limited and temporary arrangements made for the Ladies' Court Dinner once a year. Now, their Cloak Room is fully up to modern standards and the greatly increased lettings speak for themselves.

The Exhibition foreshadowed in 1950 was brought off with real success in August 1951. In this year of the great South Bank Exhibition, London had more visitors than in any year since the war and organizations of all kinds were 'on show'. Sidney Hodgson once more produced an interesting selection of our treasures, including much of the Company's plate, the famous Registers—some over 300 years old showing the 'Entry' of certain of Shakespeare's plays—and the model of the Barge attracted much attention. He also had help from the professional skill of Cuthbert Graseman, formerly Publicity Manager of the Southern Railway, in the actual display of the exhibits and in gaining some Press interest for the affair. It was opened by Sir Percy Greenaway in his capacity of Acting Lord Mayor and was attended by 3,585 visitors, including many from overseas. The Livery Committee, with members of the Court, did good work in arranging for a rota of members to hold 'vigil' in the Exhibition, both to answer questions and for reasons of security.

On personal matters, it was impressive for the Court to find that while it still had two former Lord Mayors of London in its midst, Sir Percy Greenaway and Sir George Wilkinson, both of whom had frequently to act for Sir Leslie Boyce during his illness, Denis Truscott, who had been elected to the Court on becoming an Alderman in 1948, was now elected to the office of Sheriff. This was to foreshadow the considerable distinction of the Company providing three Lord Mayors within the comparatively short span of twenty-six years: quite an achievement, it might be held, for one Livery Company among more than eighty.

In the same year also, it became possible at last to provide gowns once more for the entire Court, though funds enabled only those for Master and Wardens to be fur-trimmed. The additional purchase tax payable upon the fur at that time meant that the ordinary Assistants had to be content with scarlet edging, the idea being that fur could be added later when there might be some change in taxation. In fact, this has never been done: the scarlet is not lacking in dignity and, over the years, more than one member of the Court has been thankful not to find himself any more thickly clad on a hot summer's day! Incidentally, the author—during his Mastership in 1972—and partly to provide a slightly less heavy and also more colourful garment—presented a new style of Master's gown which embodied the Company colours of blue and gold. The idea was followed up by the Wardens of the period, Dr G. L. Riddell and Alan Greenaway, who gave new Wardens' gowns.

In 1952 one of the Court places promised in 1933 to some member of the Newspapermakers, was filled by the 'call' to John Betts, who took his seat in November of that year. One time editor of the *City Press*, he was an interesting character, well versed in, and a stickler for, Company tradition; no meeting he attended normally went through without pointed contributions from him and it might perhaps be said that he was born to keep any chairman 'on his toes'. In due time he served as Master and during the years immediately after the sale of the Ludgate Hill property when we were well 'in funds', Company functions were distinctly cheered by his liking always to have champagne available.

Another significant name to appear on the Court at the same time was that of John Mylne Rivington. His portrait is the latest to be hung in the Court Room to the left of the fireplace. His great services to the Company in the supervision, with the future Clerk Patrick Wells, of all the legal complexities of the 'extinguishment' of the English Stock, then as Master and as Treasurer will be described later.

In 1953 it was found possible to manage another Dinner for the Livery in the Hall, though there was still no Court Room; also the third of the 'At Homes' for the Livery was held in January—a modest affair but at least a worthwhile attempt to give members a chance to meet and discuss their interests. Also that year came the first of the most welcome visits of Queen Elizabeth the Queen Mother with 'the Friends of St Paul's'. Now a regular date in our Calendar, this follows the special afternoon service in the Cathedral after which Her Majesty, leaving first, comes straight to the Hall, to be greeted by the Master and 'His Lady' and given a little quiet refreshment before joining some 200 of the 'Friends' in the Hall. Then boys from the Cathedral choir sing gloriously a few unaccompanied items, conducted by the organist. All is then semi-informal as the Queen Mother moves easily from one to another of the several groups which have formed around the Hall. Her Majesty must now have fulfilled this engagement well over twenty times, but when last seen at close quarters in recent years, she gave the unfaltering impression of enjoyment of every detail and interest in all whom she met.

The Ash Wednesday Service in St Faith's, in the crypt of St Paul's, was by then fully re-established, as was the annual visit to Hendon Church to inspect the grave of Richard Johnson (and to listen to the immortal sermon on *Vita humana bulla est*).

The whole of the period of the Mastership of William Will 1953–54 was taken up with preparation for the rebuilding. The much-coveted licence for both kitchens and the whole Court Room was at last obtained, but then a totally unexpected obstacle appeared: the Dean and Chapter of St Paul's, who control the land and the beautiful old houses immediately to the north of our premises, lodged some objection to the Court Room north wall and roof being replaced. Not until July 1954 were the troubles resolved and final preparations made for the start of the work. One consolation was that, as in the case of the Hall, the original designs of walls and ceiling of the Court Room were still available so that they could be reproduced by contemporary craftsmen. So, the room which to many is the most attractive part of all our buildings, was restored to its full splendour and did, indeed, look finer than anyone could remember it in pre-war days. There must be few newcomers, be they apprentices, those coming to take up their Freedom or the Livery, or the visitor taking his drink there before a dinner, who are not struck by its fine proportions, yet by the sense of intimacy it can give to any gathering. Dating originally from 1670, the interior shows an unusual example of the Jacobean style of interior decoration in its more refined stage before it gave way to the greater elegance and delicacy of the Georgian age. The soft colour of the exterior brickwork is in keeping with the surroundings, which include the north wall of the old church of St Martin-within-Ludgate. Thus was the famous 'garden where the heretical books were burnt' made neat and tidy once more, and its lovely plane tree continues to flourish.

Though the exterior of the Hall and the adjoining buildings were now restored, there was still much to be done inside before it could once again be fully used. In 1954 another of the pioneer Livery Committeemen, Richard A. Austen-Leigh, who had been their first Chairman, became Master. Sadly, his health was then deteriorating, functions could still not be held in the Hall, and altogether he, who had done much in his younger days for the future well-being of the Company, could not enjoy his Mastership to the full. However, by the following year the whole west wing, including the kitchens, was complete and the architect, Geoffrey Gurney, and his contractors were rightly commended by the Master, William Penman, for their fine workmanship.

The important section of interior reconstruction still needed was below, and the approach to, the Stock Room. The area involved included the old basement offices used then by the Clerk and the Beadle, who had to be housed temporarily in the Stock Room, while part of the Hall had to do duty as a store-room—one more period of great inconvenience, but cheerfully faced by those most concerned. The building work involved was considerable, as it included entirely new cloak-rooms for both men and women as well as the reconstruction of the handsome staircase and landing leading up to the Stock Room. Still, it was not practicable to hold a dinner in the Hall and though one for the Livery was given in the Hall of the Vintners' Company, the attendance was disappointing, clear evidence, it would seem, of Stationers' longing to be back in their own Hall—and the time was approaching.

In William Penman's year the Court was kept well employed. This may have been due, in part, to the drive of an exceptionally able Master who was an Actuary of wide experience, but a great many new questions arose as the Company prepared to become fully operational once again and hoped, indeed, to do more than in the past.

The decision in 1956 of the Clerk, Reginald Rivington, not to seek re-election would have caused upheaval. He had held the office since 1916, was 75 years of age, and despite the handicap of considerable lameness due to arthritis, remained very much in possession of all his faculties. To many it must have seemed 'impossible to imagine the Company without him'. He had given fifty years of most devoted service, extending over two World Wars, and had carried the Company through a long period when funds were short and problems abounded. Mr Rivington had, moreover, accomplished it all as a part-time job.

In the event, a most fortunate choice of successor was made in Patrick Wells. He had held RAF Staff appointments during the last war and as a partner in a very old firm of solicitors he already had valuable City connections. April 1957, when he took up his duties with us, was the start of a crucial time in the Company's history. As will be seen, the Ludgate Hill property sale was soon to take place and thereafter the complex negotiations were to begin for the subsequent presentation to Parliament of the Bill for the extinguishment of the English Stock. As Clerk and Legal Adviser to the Company, Mr Wells undertook an exceptional load of work in the research and 'devilling' to assist the Treasurer, J. M. Rivington, in preparation of the case for Counsel of the Bill to Parliament. Furthermore, he had the entire conduct of the Parliamentary proceedings in conjunction with the Parliamentary Agents.

Under the new conditions in which the Clerkship was to become a full-time job and was paid accordingly, opportunity was taken to transfer the Registry from the Clerk to the Company, and a new scale of fees was fixed; previously they had been retained by the Clerk as some addition to his modest remuneration for the part-time occupation. As an aside, it is remarkable that so many books were still registered at our Hall more than forty years after it ceased to be a condition of copyright. The practice continues unabated today. Now, it has proved necessary to increase the scale of fees still further owing to the amount of clerical work involved, including provision of certified copies of the 'entry'. For a large number of publications, often privately issued and quite outside the channels of the Book Trade, firm and independent evidence of the date of publication by the stated party can be valuable.

The Court was also concerned with the new 'Instrument'

and Articles of Government made by the Minister of Education under the famous Education Act of 1944 as it affected the Stationers' School at Hornsey. Under it the Company had to appoint twelve Governors out of a total of eighteen instead of the former eight Governors out of nineteen. To avoid the School losing the services of four valued Governors formerly appointed by the Local Authorities, the Court agreed that on the first occasion it should appoint four of the existing appointees of the Local Councils. The gesture was much appreciated by the School Board, but much greater changes in future years could be expected.

A new and increased scale of fees for the letting of the Hall and Stock Room was decided upon, with small reductions for members of the Company taking them for parties of their own; security arrangements for all our valuable archives were much tightened up; the basis upon which it was intended, in the future, to pay pensions to the staff was agreed; and lastly it was decided, as from 1957, to have four Renter Wardens each year instead of the former two. Not that the duties are so onerous—far from it—but the office is one which for one year brings the Liveryman, after about ten years, into closer touch with Company affairs and gives him also the chance to meet members of the Court at lunch once a month. As well as proving instructive to many, the experience can be most enjoyable, and it is good that it should be shared by a larger number than formerly. Renter Wardens today also play more part at the moments of ceremony: at Livery Dinners, for example, their presence in the Stock Room is most valuable. While Master and Wardens are closely held to the ritual handshakes of reception, many a Renter Warden has given care to some important guest and every Master must have been grateful for their unseen hands which remove his fur-trimmed gown immediately Grace has been said, and he is then less thickly clad for the anxious time ahead of him!

The Livery Committee became increasingly active and the Master was able to report the pleasure of 'attending several enjoyable functions' organized by it, of which more is described elsewhere; the point here is simply that the new growth of a generation before had now established itself confidently and had swung into action again as soon as possible after the war. It should also be mentioned that after the untimely death of Mr Price in 1952, Mr and Mrs J. E. Nevill had been appointed in his place, forming an admirable partnership, with the latter proving herself an excellent cook. Mr Nevill was also an expert bowls player, captaining a City team in which more than one member of the Court enjoyed playing.

On Saturday, 4 May 1957, the 400th Anniversary of the granting of our Second Royal Charter was celebrated by a full Livery Dinner in the completely restored Hall with all its ancillary parts in working order. The Lord Mayor, Colonel Sir Cullum Welch, formally declared the Hall open and another distinguished guest was the Prime Minister, Harold Macmillan, who had accepted the Honorary Freedom and Livery of the Company in the previous year. This had taken place in the midst of the Suez crisis and Mr Macmillan had been obliged to cut short his time with us at the ceremony in order to dash back to Downing Street; he was then Chancellor of the Exchequer.

That Charter Dinner was truly memorable for those who attended it. They could feel, on the fine spring evening, that at long last, after seventeen years, the Stationers' Company was fully in action once more and able to show its traditional hospitality. The pleasure of any daylight function in the Hall then was enhanced by the exceptional beauty of the dome of St Paul's as seen from the east windows, before the new buildings arose on our former site in Ave Maria Lane. All that flowed from that great event belongs to our next chapter, but it was foreshadowed in 1957 by the Master, Cuthbert Graseman. He pointed out to members that, thanks to the hard work of previous Masters, the time was then within sight when planning permission would be granted to build on that most valuable strip of land, with the frontage on Ludgate Hill, and upon it depended the future prosperity of the Company.

CHAPTER FIVE

The Property Sale

AS READERS OF Blagden's history will be well aware, the English Stock of the Company had its origins in the trading activities of the seventeenth century, when it received the royal grant of a monopoly to 'ymprint the Bookes of private prayers, prymers, psalters and psalmes in English or Latin, & Almanrackes and Prognosticacõns wthin this Realme'. This grew into a prosperous book-producing and bookselling organization run from Stationers' Hall and during the years of the monopolies substantial profits were easily achieved. Subsequently income from the 'Stock'—which had produced originally the largest single item in the receipts—dwindled, even by 1900, to a mere £362—whereas the rents received were far and away the main source of income. Until 1961, however, the English Stock was the name still given to the bulk of the Company's assets and to serve upon the Stock Board was one of the more interesting appointments which might come to a Liveryman provided he had taken up a share when offered to him. Prior to that year one was called upon to pay £80 for a Yeomanry share, £160 for a Livery share, and £320 for a Court share, and in the far-off days when a regular 12½ per cent dividend had been paid, it was a most attractive investment. (The fact that such a rate was kept up long after the finances of the Company had ceased to justify it did not appear to disturb the Assistants of the last century, but that is past history!)

What concerns us here is that it was the Stock Board which had considerable responsibility for the Company's properties and their future development, and it was particularly fortunate that Sir George Wilkinson was then its Treasurer. His long and

successful business career, culminating in his term as Lord
Mayor, had given him exceptional knowledge of the City and
he was accustomed to the handling of financial affairs on a large
scale. As will be seen, his contributions to discussion at Stock
Board meetings became of increasing interest in the immediate
post-war years when plans were formulated for the rebuilding
of the area around St Paul's, including Paternoster Row and the
vicinity of Stationers' Hall Court.

The previous Chapter has recorded many achievements in
the efforts of the Company to recover from the losses and
disorder of the War. As the 1950s drew towards their end
many could look back in thankfulness to the advancement in
living standards and the general increase in supplies of all sorts—
not least paper!—which had taken place since the end of the
war, when most commodities, be they food, clothes, petrol, or
building materials, were strictly rationed. People in their
thirties today would, however, be much surprised if they
could be suddenly translated even to the London of 1959. Very
few 'high-rise' buildings were then in evidence and innumerable
great empty gaps between the City offices still marked the
places where bombs had fallen.

Approaching Stationers' Hall down Warwick Lane, from
Newgate Street, one still had that superb, unobstructed view of
the entire north side of St Paul's Cathedral, which had been
laid bare suddenly in December 1940 by the destruction of
Paternoster Row. Hodder and Stoughton's staff maintained a
beautiful little garden at the corner of Warwick Square on the
empty land on which part of their offices had stood before the
Blitz. In Ave Maria Lane one looked straight across to Stationers' Hall, where there had been the large building occupied by
Simpkin Marshall, and adjoining it were the ruins of the office
block and shops which the Company had owned on Ludgate
Hill. This brief dissertation on the London scene of nearly
twenty years ago is just to bring home to the reader that, despite
the great progress in rebuilding our Hall, the vital source of
future revenue in our freehold land remained untapped and
unexploited. Victor Penman, however, was able to state in his

Master's Report for 1957–58 that during his year the Court had made important decisions concerning the Company's property and he emphasized the progress made on the Planning Application for the development of the still vacant sites on Ludgate Hill and Ave Maria Lane. While at first sight it might seem extraordinary that there should have been any hesitation about permission being granted to replace in modern form a commercial building on Ludgate Hill, the matter was complicated by the nearness to St Paul's.

The famous architect Sir William Holford was responsible for the rebuilding plan of that whole area of the Cathedral precincts and, understandably, no one section could be rebuilt without reference to the entire scheme. The proposed realignment of Ave Maria Lane, where it enters Ludgate Hill, was naturally a key question in relation to the sort of building which might be permitted on our site immediately to the west. Members of the Stationers' Company who approach the Hall on foot, up Ludgate Hill, must find it difficult to forgive the planning official who sanctioned that ugly protrusion of the new building on the east corner of the Lane—which now obscures more of the west front of the Cathedral than in pre-war days—but that is not on the Company's former land and was no concern of ours.

After many delays and disappointments and, at one stage, an adverse decision of the Planning Committee of the then London County Council, Mr Penman could report that 'there are definite signs that approval of the Company's building plan now in the hands of Sir William Holford will receive sanction in the near future'. Anyone with experience of such matters will at once appreciate that if the land were to be sold, it was vital for us to be able to offer it *with* planning permission already granted. Only thus could the maximum price be obtained for what was the most valuable single part of our heritage.

Upon the Court and the Stock Board much discussion took place over many sessions. Not many of those present would have had experience of monetary dealings running far into six figures and still fewer realized the almost astronomical rise which was to take place in City land values. Here Sir George Wilkinson, as Treasurer of the English Stock, was an invaluable mentor and it was he who first emphasized the fact that the real money was to be made by those who developed the site, actually paying for and owning the building which was to be erected on it. Until then, probably most of those present looked no further than to the possession of the handsome capital sum anticipated from the sale of the freehold. It is fair to say that, apart from those actually engaged in 'property dealing, in those days the average man had little conception of either the likely rate of inflation to come or of the extent to which property would prove to be the best 'hedge' against it.

When this particular point was made by the Company's Surveyors, at a meeting of the old English Stock Board, Sir George Wilkinson was after it at once. 'This whets my appetite', he said and encouraged the meeting to consider carefully whether it might not be possible to raise the capital needed for us to erect our own building on Ludgate Hill and continue to own that irreplaceable piece of real estate. It was a dazzling prospect. With the contacts possessed by various members, it would have been by no means impossible to raise the substantial capital needed. Some might conceivably have agreed to low-interest loans and, anyhow, with the security of a London City freehold, loans on ordinary commercial terms could have been raised from insurance companies or other financial institutions.

There are many people who might have said that it was a fundamental mistake for the Company to have contemplated the sale of freehold property in such a prominent position. In principle they were quite right, but to adhere to that course would have involved the Company in a tremendous business undertaking on a scale for which it was quite unfitted. While some person, or organization, could doubtless have been employed, at a price, to deal with all the complexities of building and subsequently the letting of such premises, it was the apparent length of time which must elapse before any net income could accrue to the Company which proved the stumbling-block.

Here the actuarial expertise of William Penman ensured that the cold facts were fully revealed in a masterly statement. It clearly demonstrated how much the building was likely to cost, the anticipated income from rents, and the number of years over which such income must be devoted almost wholly to the repayment of the initial loan, estimated then at about £500,000. (Sale of the site was assumed, at *that* stage, to bring in about £200,000.)

With the prospect, at the time, of having to face another twenty years or more without appreciable income the Court and Livery took the view that it was impracticable for the Company to tackle the development itself. Looking back twenty years, with our knowledge of how relatively modest the cost of building, compared to 1977, would have been then, and the substantial rent increases which could have been made in the meantime, one cannot but feel that a unique opportunity was missed. The contrary opinion has been abundantly justified by the rise in property values since 1957 and in the Company's portfolio of investments the Property shares have increased sixfold in price, representing one of our best investments in terms of capital appreciation.

Against this it must be remembered that the Court was very much aware that for eighteen years the average Liveryman had had very little for his money; twelve years had gone by since the end of the war, dinners were still few and far between, and there were implied promises that soon we should be more prosperous and that there would be 'more doing' in every way. One can readily see how strong was the impulse to realize the Property Asset then and there, investing it prudently, and not to embark upon the possibly hazardous, and undoubtedly time-consuming, business of fresh building and its management. To put in yet another word in defence of those who made the decision to sell, it should be mentioned that in the immediate pre-war years there had been much un-let office space in London. At least one of those present on the Stock Board in the

1950s could recall a well-placed building, completed in 1931, in which two of the five floors remained unoccupied for eight years. Now, again in 1977, there are many 'To Let' boards to be seen in the City.

Once the final decision to sell had been taken, 'the Site Sub-Committee' was appointed and its responsible task was in the capable hands of the Master for 1958–59, George P. Simon, of the *Daily Telegraph*, Sir George Wilkinson, and William and Victor Penman, the last three being Past Masters. No one then guessed what figure was to emerge as the purchase price. The leading firm of estate agents, with much experience of City property, acting as the Company's advisers, arrived at the figure of about £200,000 as the likely market value. Attractive as this might have appeared, it would have yielded no more than £10,000 per annum at 5 per cent, from which tax was of course deductible. (Though substantially more than our pre-war income, it would not have enabled us to expand our activities even in 1958: in fact, today, our annual expenditure is about seven times that amount.)

Wishing to obtain the best offer possible, the Sub-Committee advertised the site, inviting offers of £285,000 or over. Eleven such offers were received, whereupon the would-be purchasers were all invited to send in further offers in sealed envelopes, to be opened in Stationers' Hall at noon on 8 April 1959 in the presence of the parties concerned and their advisers. To the enormous gratification of Master, Wardens, and Committee the highest bid came out at well above three times the original estimated figure. The £663,000 paid by the Colonial Mutual Life Assurance Society Ltd was, as Mr Simon stated, 'quite beyond the expectations of the Court and its advisers'. At this figure, representing £1,750,000 per acre, the transaction was then believed to be the highest price ever paid for land in the City of London.

For an overseas company seeking a prestige site, in the shadow of St Paul's, it was obviously extremely attractive and a very fine stroke of business. At the same time one is left marvelling at the strange elements of chance: how nearly we might, on professional advice, have accepted a much lower offer; how exceptionally fortunate we were to have just then in the top levels of the Court men of such calibre and wide business experience as George Simon and Sir George Wilkinson, and that a rich Company from the Antipodes should have been in the property market just at the right moment—small wonder that there is said to have been a certain popping of champagne corks in the Court Room on 8 May 1959, the day on which the transaction was completed.

Some account of the Company's investment policies is given later. Here it is enough to remark that the immediate prospect of an income of some £30,000 per annum transformed the outlook. It also brought new problems, but of an interesting nature and, all in all, fresh life was infused into the whole organization.

That great year of 1959, besides bringing one of the most beautiful summers on record, showed also the full potentialities of our Hall, when it could be fully operational. The Master attended more than sixty functions in it. The great majority were those of outside organizations which were, of course, making a further and useful addition to our revenue. His own connections, almost certainly, led to the famous Grolier Club of New York, with its many literary associations, holding a most impressive function in Stationers' Hall, at which Lord Salisbury and the President of the Board of Trade were present. Another unusual gathering was that of the Permanent Way Institution of Great Britain, arising doubtless from Cuthbert Graseman's railway associations.

The Company's continual wish to assist and support the Trades of our Guild was given effect with the 'Layton Awards Exhibition' for Printing. This was held for a week in the Hall and it was declared open by Lord Hailsham. The activities of the Livery Committee that year, besides running a Ball and other social functions, included also an enterprising invitation to Sir William Haley, then Director General of the BBC, to lecture on 'The Effects of Television on the Crafts of the Stationers and Newspaper Makers Company'. The Committee also earned the gratitude of future speakers in our Hall by presenting to the Court a solid and particularly well-designed oak reading-desk in commemoration of the Quater-centenary of the Company. That somewhat capricious device of sound equipment was also provided—an inevitable expectation by those hiring the Hall (but perpetual trap for the unwary speaker if he does not keep exactly the right distance from the microphone!).

Meanwhile the Muniment Room was used increasingly by Professors of English from American universities, by other students and research workers, and constantly by the late Cyprian Blagden while working on his authoritative history of the Company in its earlier days. Other subjects for research at that time were Samuel Richardson, Benjamin Franklin, and William Strahan—indicating the scope and variety of the records in our care. Among the several small exhibitions of our Court Books and Registers, kindly arranged by Sidney Hodgson, was one for the Magistrates' Association, for which there was a large attendance. Though nearing his ninetieth year, Mr Hodgson retained astonishing vitality and his full knowledge of all the Company Records was undiminished; he was gifted with quite exceptional powers, continuing to give valuable advice on the Company's Records to the end of his life.

An item of domestic interest for that year was the retirement of another loyal and friendly servant of the Company, Ernest Mettrop, who, it will be remembered, succeeded William Poulten as Beadle in 1940. He had come straight into the worst times of our history, in terms of constant upheaval, inconvenience, and discomfort. He carried on, in Mr Simon's words, 'in an exemplary manner despite the damage to the premises and the many and varied difficulties arising from the years of rebuilding and restoration'. He was also a musician, specializing in choral singing, and more than once his choir provided entertainment at Livery Dinners. A kindly and unflappable man, it was a shame that he did not remain with us long enough to enjoy the much greater convenience of the new offices which were soon to be fitted out in the old warehouse on the west side of the garden.

Sir Denis Truscott, having been one of the youngest-ever of Lord Mayors of London in 1957, became for 1959-60 one of the youngest Masters of our Company. Whatever may have been his personal feelings at the time, there can be no doubt it was fortunate for us that for the interesting but intricate problems ahead the Company should have had, in Sir Denis, a man in the prime of life, backed by wide experience of City matters.

The problem which dominated his year and that of his successor was the future of the English Stock following the sale of the property. A very brief outline of the origins of this Stock was given at the start of this chapter. That it had remained for so long separate and apart from the unfettered capital of the Company was in itself largely an anachronism. Historical reasons, coupled maybe with some sentimental feelings, had caused reluctance in abolishing the traditional operation of the Company, which was, after all, unique in the life of a Livery Company. For many years past the problem had been seen as a formidable one, largely because of the difficulties of construing in the twentieth century bye-laws which had been drawn up in 1681 for the government of the English Stock.

After prolonged and careful deliberation the Court decided that a Constitutional Committee must be set up, with the Clerk as legal adviser, to examine the whole position and make recommendations about the future of the Stock. Following very thorough consideration, and having obtained the opinion of leading Counsel, the Committee submitted its report. This strongly advised that steps be taken to 'wind up' the stock forthwith and, in accordance with Counsel's opinion, recommended that the only practical course open to the Company was to apply for a private Act of Parliament dealing with and clearing up the situation. A special meeting of the Livery was held on 22 April 1960, at which the situation was fully explained, the above course was agreed, and instructions were given for the laborious and expensive process of the preparation of the private Bill. A small but high-powered Committee consisting of Master and Wardens, Sir Denis Truscott, William Penman, and John Mylne Rivington, drafted the crucial letter which, after approval by Counsel, was sent out to all the Livery in July. A reassuring response was received and the Bill was actually lodged in Parliament by 25 November 1960—commendably quick work in all the circumstances, reflecting great credit on J. M. Rivington and Patrick Wells.

Two of the terms in the Bill which required special consideration were first the charitable provision which replaced the existing liability under the bye-laws of the English Stock to provide the sum of £200 per annum for the poor of the Company. Second was the contentious matter of the compensation to be paid to Stockholders and other Liverymen on the Roll of the Livery at the date of the redemption, and extinguishment of the English Stock; in calculating any such amount one had to bear in mind their loss of future dividends on the winding-up of the Stock.

The first point was settled by the Court's decision to create a fund of £25,000, with power for the charitable use of the income thereof. The second was the cause of an unfortunate division of opinion on the Court: a small but well-informed minority felt strongly that the existing holders of the Stock were entitled to be treated on a basis similar to that of the holders of ordinary shares at the winding-up, or 'take-over', of a limited company. In view of the great sum paid for the Stationers' main asset, the Ludgate Hill site, this could have meant a very substantial profit, in the form of a capital payment, for those fortunate enough to be holding any of the English Stock at that time.

Since 1939 the return on the Stock had been negligible and one had paid for a share principally to establish one's seniority, and to show practical interest in the Company. There must have been few who latterly ever regarded such shares as likely to prove a profitable investment. The £663,000 'windfall' from the property sale was the very heart and core of our heritage; such a stupendous piece of good fortune was unlikely ever to come our way again; and it was the majority view that the capital must be nurtured with the greatest care so as to provide income and growth for the future. This is not to say that, after our years in the wilderness, more than one of us did not look momentarily, with some longing, at the enticing terms suggested in the minority proposals, involving a substantial capital payment to stockholders, but to all but three of the stockholders there was never any real doubt as to the more prudent course for the future of the Company. (Before the dispute and as some compensation for the many years in which no dividend had been paid, a special 50 per cent dividend was paid soon after the sale of the property.)

The alternative proposal adopted was that now in being, by which the holders of the original shares were repaid their Stock at par and then received annuities of £16 for Yeomanry, £32 for Livery, and £64 for Court denominations. This did not apply to those who joined the Company after 1961, when the English Stock was 'extinguished'. Thus, although on the death of one of the original annuitants, or his widow, his entitlement passes to the next Liveryman in the category eligible to succeed to it, the number *is* decreasing all the time. Whereas there were originally, in addition to Court Assistants, 330 Liverymen (or their widows) entitled to annuities in due course, there are now only about 140. It will, of course, be many years before all of them have died, but at least it is not an unlimited liability for the Company.

In recent years many annuitants have agreed that they should, at least temporarily, waive their rights annually to help the Company's finances during the worst period of inflation; one dare not contemplate what the original 'dissidents' would have thought about this, but the matter is now past history. The conclusion of this honest but strongly held difference of opinion, stemming from the Court, can best be recalled in the words of James Ousey, Master in 1960–61:

Copies of the proposed Bill were circulated to all the Livery on January 6th 1961, and the required Statutory Meetings of the Stockholders and Liverymen were held in the Hall on January 31st 1961 at which on a ballot of stockholders 99 . . . voted in favour of the Bill and three against, as did 232 of the Liverymen present or voting by proxy and three against, on the subsequent ballot of the Livery. Upon these figures it was hoped that the Bill would have a smooth passage through Parliament, but unhappily . . . the proceedings were contested in the House of Lords, with consequent heavy expense to the Company.

The one practical result of the minority action was that, at the suggestion of Their Lordships, the Bill was amended to give the Court unfettered discretion to increase the rate of the annuities in any year should it be deemed expedient. At length the Bill so amended became an Act of Parliament on 19 July 1961.

James Ousey was a remarkable character among our Masters: a tall, handsome, white-haired figure nearly eighty years of age, he had to travel up from Bishopsteignton in Devonshire for every meeting and his customary tweeds brought a not unwelcome air of the countryside with him. Some found him irascible, and, perhaps, unduly outspoken, but he had severe difficulties during his year, resulting partly from the fact that William Penman, then Treasurer of the Company, was in opposition to the general view on the annuities. Certainly it is to the credit of the Master that the problems were faced unflinchingly and ultimately resolved.

There were several other good developments in his year: the ties with the Royal Marines were further strengthened, Senior Officers being invited to Livery functions, and a special reception was held for Junior Officers at which Cuthbert Graseman gave a talk on our history and the purpose of the Company. The then Commandant-General, Sir Ian Riches, KCB, reciprocated by entertaining the Court to a dinner held in honour of the Company at the Royal Marine Barracks, Eastney, near Portsmouth. All those privileged to attend, the Master commented, 'will long remember the wonderful hospitality extended to them on that occasion'. The invitation has been repeated for many subsequent Masters, all of whom would undoubtedly concur with Mr Ousey's view. General Riches attended the Civic Dinner in 1961, in accordance with the then well-established practice of his predecessors. He also gave great pleasure by accepting the invitation to one of the Livery Lunches and giving a particularly interesting account of the Royal Marines.

The advantages in 1949 of our 'adoption' of that most distinguished Corps may not have been at once obvious, but there was no doubt of the mutual pleasure and interest which it engendered. It is interesting that the success of that Lunch should have prompted one of the very few 'bouquets' to the Livery Committee to be found in Masters' Reports. The Committee was said to have been very well served by its then Chairman, Dr G. L. Riddell (and no wonder!); also that the Livery Representatives, Mr H. V. B. Dove and Mr A. G. L. Atkinson, had been of much assistance to the Court. A small matter, perhaps, but good testimony to the distance travelled since 1920 and a great tribute to the twenty-seven years' former secretaryship of Dr Riddell and the wise advice he had tendered to a succession of Chairmen, before his very proper elevation to that position himself.

The year 1960 saw the publication of Cyprian Blagden's *The Stationers' Company* by George Allen & Unwin Ltd. Never viewed as exactly a money-maker by its publishers, it nevertheless covered its costs, thanks in part to an order for a few hundred copies from Harvard University Press and to the sale of a small remainder of the stock at a reduced price to the Stationers' Company. It may not seem the lightest of entertainment for the general reader, but it is a scholarly work and it does deal in detail with those years of the Company's greatest influence as well as providing a full description of the original English Stock, a trading concern unique for a City Guild. The continuing interest of Blagden to scholars has been further recognized by its 1977 reprinting in the United States.

Let this chapter which has recorded much solid progress in

post-war recovery conclude with one more restoration of a happy pre-war function, the Court and Ladies' Dinner. It had not been held for over twenty years, its resumption having been delayed by the need to rebuild the Court Room, the kitchen, and the accommodation for ladies. Traditionally it comes about the middle of May when our plane tree can look its very best on a sunny evening and asparagus is in season! Few Masters can have failed to enjoy it to the utmost: no formal business is involved, just a short speech of welcome to which one of the ladies replies and, for the rest, it is a purely social gathering of friends in the most beautiful of the rooms at Stationers' Hall. For the Master it signals almost the end of his term of office and for James Ousey it must have meant an enjoyable conclusion to what had earlier been a most difficult year.

CHAPTER SIX

The New Prosperity 1960–64

W ITH THE BANKING of that cheque for £663,000 it was easy for some to imagine that our problems were solved and that there would be in future unlimited money available for all manner of new developments. It was, of course, vital that it should be used positively and with imagination for the long-term benefit of the Stationers' Company and, so far as possible, to assist the 'Trades of the Guild' in ways beyond those of ordinary, day-to-day commercial activities. Plans had to be made with the greatest care.

The main considerations to which the Finance Committee had to address itself may be summarized as follows:

(1) The actual forms of investment for the Capital sum.
(2) What further expenditure should be permitted upon the Establishment?
(3) How best to reorganize the Charities?
(4) Appropriate forms of assistance to the Company's School at Hornsey.
(5) Last but by no means least, future expenditure upon functions of all kinds in the Hall, social and for the 'Trades'.

To take them in order, first came the absorbing question of investments, and for this an Investment Sub-Committee was set up. It now meets with the Company's stockbroker, Philip Curtis, a senior partner in the firm of Fielding, Newson-Smith (introduced to the Company through one of Patrick Wells's connections). In the weeks between these meetings the Com-

pany Treasurer is in frequent touch with Mr Curtis and, when
urgently necessary, changes in the investments can be made on
the authority of Master and Treasurer alone.

From the outset in 1960, the principle agreed was to invest
one-third of the funds in gilt-edged, one-third in equity stocks,
and the remaining third in real estate. While the good yield of
the 'gilts' was sought after, it was realized that the Company
must take a long view and that the money then at our dispsoal
was the fruit of investment made over 300 years before. It was
essential therefore to be looking a century ahead and to have
in mind always the 'growth' potential of at least two-thirds of
the portfolio. Even in the early 1960s one was sufficiently aware
of inflation to realize that the Company's capital must be
invested largely in the ordinary shares of sound businesses
which could be expected to go on growing over the years.

On the early Investment Sub-Committee there were some
who would have preferred to see a larger proportion of the
funds put into those supposedly 'safe' fixed-interest Government stocks which yielded higher rates of interest. It was
pleasant enough to see the income produced in this way—
higher than it would have been from an equivalent investment
in equities. Five years later, however, the amount of income
remained static, while scores of such Government stocks had
declined sharply in capital value. War Loan and the once time-
honoured Consolidated Stock ('Consols') were two cases in
point and the accounts of many public bodies, including even
the great Restoration Fund of St Paul's, were littered with
examples of heavy capital losses on such investments.

Carefully selected equities, though producing a lower yield
at the outset, almost invariably grew in value at that time and,
with increased dividends, the income from them rose. The
emphasis, of course, is on the care and expertise with which the
companies are selected for investment. In 1977 the Company's
investment income was more than double what it was in the
early 1960s, a result which could not have been achieved from
investment in the fixed-interest gilt-edged stocks. The original
intention to invest in some real estate was not carried out, but

in addition to one property company several of our other holdings had a considerable property element in their assets.

Establishment costs of the Company inevitably rose, but were kept within reasonable limits. Some upward revision of salaries was overdue because they had been inevitably held back during the years of financial stringency; also the Clerk, Patrick Wells, was by then undertaking full-time duties for the Company; his original appointment, as in the case of Reginald Rivington, had been on a part-time basis. He had been joined by Stanley Osborne, as his assistant, in 1959, after the retirement of Ernest Mettrop. Curiously enough, in Stanley Osborne the Company again had the benefit of an experienced musician able to play a church organ for the occasional Company service and to provide pleasant piano music sometimes for the Ladies' Court Dinner. His immaculate handwriting of the Court Order Books over more than fifteen years was to ease the task of anyone studying Stationers' history of that period and he also kept the Registry Records of all publications 'entered at Stationers' Hall'.

Expenditure under this heading did not end with salary increases. It had long been recognized that the office accommodation was unworthy, and what may have been passable in earlier years with part-time staff was quite inadequate under modern conditions. What had once been warehouses on the west side of the garden had been used latterly for the dwindling supplies of the English [book] Stock, mainly copies of Carey's *Gradus* and a few issues of the old Almanacs. Also, part of it had been let to a publisher, Butterworths. This arrangement was terminated, the building cleared, and the interior rebuilt into three modern offices and lavatories: thus was created the convenient staff block as we now know it. Until some ten years later there was no internal communication with the Hall and in the interval there had to be a somewhat unsightly iron staircase, the only direct access from the offices up, via a french window, into the Court Room. The improved lay-out of today, with internal stairs, had to await the creation of the Master's Room in 1971.

The third of the aforementioned considerations, the Charities, was dealt with at first by the allocation of £25,000 in accordance with the terms of the Bill under which the English Stock was wound up. This, added to other Charity funds already held by the Company, has built up to over £60,000 and the investment of part in the well-known Charifund, covering certain equity stocks, has provided the chance for some growth. At the same time it has, of course, ensured that we have been able to raise the amounts of the pensions paid to the needy Freemen and their widows who have some assistance from the Company.

As for the Stationers' School, its changed status after the 1944 Education Act, to which reference was made in Chapter 4, relieved the Company of some, but not all, of the weight of financial responsibility. More is said about this later.

The fifth item mentioned above, functions in the Hall, primarily to assist the Trades, was not the subject of any special allocation from the funds, but the easier financial circumstances enabled the Court to accept rather more readily proposals made from time to time for the entertainment of societies or groups, sometimes from overseas, who wished to visit the Hall and to hold their meetings in it. One example of this was the National Library Week organized by the Library Association and the Publishers' Association with the help of booksellers; also, at the time of the World Book Fair at Earls Court in 1964, a reception was given for all the exhibitors from foreign countries. Hospitality was also offered more readily on other similar occasions and the Hall was used in ways which justify completely the effort and expense involved in its upkeep. It becomes the ideal *venue* for so many of such gatherings and leaves foreign visitors, in particular, delighted to participate in a small slice of our history and traditions.

In 1962, the year of the Mastership of W. H. Young, the Court decided to make an annual grant of £100 to the Livery Committee and to take over responsibility and the inevitable expense involved in the organization of the Livery Lecture. This had become an annual event attracting an increasing amount of attention—sometimes being reported in the national press. However, it had been difficult for the Committee on its own always to secure the facilities of screen, projector, sound amplification, and even a satisfactory platform! (One year the lecturer had been disconcerted to find a board beneath him rise and fall slightly every time the man next to him shifted his feet—such was the uncertain quality of the temporary structure.)

The participation of the Court was more than welcome and most of these problems were then solved. There was, however, still one anxious time when need for a screen and projector had left too little space for chairs and Master George Riddell, after introducing the lecturer, found himself in his chair tipping dangerously backwards over the edge of the platform, saved only by grabbing the table in front of him and by the strong arm of David Wyndham-Smith beside him! Apart from such adventures the whole occasion was improved with a little more ceremony; Court Assistants, gowned, now occupy the front row and it has become standard practice for the lecturer always to be invited to our pleasantest form of hospitality afterwards, namely, the small dinner in the Court Room. It must, however, be remembered that the original conception of the Lecture had been that of the Livery Committee. It began at a modest level, but nowadays the audience regularly fills the Hall.

So it can be fairly claimed that the aims of the Finance Committee in 1960 have been kept in mind, and in large measure fulfilled. The rather strict economies of recent years, primarily since the oil crisis of 1973, have not seriously cut the Company's programme of significant activities.

So far in this chapter there has been reference to only one Master, W. H. Young, but although many developments in our history took place over a period spanning more than one Mastership, it proves the best method for the reader, one feels, to relate events mainly to each Master in chronological order. For 1962-63 the Livery List dispensed with the customary portrait of the incoming Master, in favour of two striking photos, one of the desolate Stationers' Hall Court in wartime,

the other showing it fully restored and viewed below the fine
sweep of the new Colonial Mutual building.

An important event of the year was the retirement of the
Headmaster of the Stationers' School, S. C. Nunn, who had
held the position since 1936. During his time he had raised its
academic standards to new heights with an ever-increasing
number of boys gaining university places. Although he had had
to deal with the wartime disturbance of evacuation of the
entire School to Wisbech, the boys prospered there and local
reports had spoken highly of the 'tone' of the School and their
good behaviour. As a gesture of appreciation the town was
presented with the Company's Silver Medal after the war. In
place of Mr Nunn was appointed R. D. Baynes, formerly
headmaster of Richmond in Yorkshire who, as all who have
had any experience of the School well know, has risen magnificently to the succession of problems experienced by a rapidly
growing school during fifteen turbulent years.

In 1963 there succeeded to the Master's Chair another man
of strong character, not easily deflected from his convictions
despite opposition, but well versed in City tradition and un-
wearied in his work for the good of the Stationers' Company.
He was the redoubtable John Betts, former editor of the *City
Press* who had entered the Company as a Newspaperman in
1933. He was the last of the five Newspapermen who had been
promised a place on the Court. The writer served with him
both on Livery Committee and later in Court. By no means
always in agreement with him, one found him ever a courteous,
as well as a 'bonnie', fighter and it was not only his chance
resemblance to my maternal grandfather which endeared him
to me. (If I may be still more personal, with him present there
seemed to be almost invariably some interesting clash of
opinion in Court with Betts going into minority opposition. In
common parlance you could put nothing 'past him' unless it
had been thoroughly thrashed out. A standing joke between us
used to be a very solicitous enquiry from me as to his health if
a Court meeting went by with no keenly—and most intelli-
gently—contested point raised by him.) He also left his mark by

establishing the custom of our always drinking champagne before Company dinners in place of sherry.

A sad event of his year was the death of his Under Warden, Major S. E. Sandle, after some months when ill-health had prevented him from carrying out his duties to the full. He had been a valiant supporter of the Livery Committee over many years and was at times an outspoken critic of the Court. It was a tragedy that he so narrowly missed the chance of serving the highest office in the Company after he had devoted much thought and effort in trying to improve its working, especially in relation to the Livery. He had also served as a Livery Representative on the Court in 1939-41.

John Betts saw to a tightening-up of the conditions of intake, with each candidate being interviewed by the Master, or one of the Wardens, as well as being vouched for by two Liverymen; the actual system has been modified in later years to a small committee of three Past Masters. The selection continues very much in the spirit of Betts's summing-up, when he stated: 'I feel we have ensured the succession of able men who, in due course, will be acceptable to the Court and worthy of the distinction of Mastership.'

A small committee set up in 1960, on which Betts took a leading part, did good work in surveying the accumulation of various possessions which had been thrown into confusion as a result of the bombing and then the rebuilding. Portraits were identified, cleaned, and rehung, while others, long overdue for attention, were treated to advantage. The initiation of all this work brought attention to the whole interior which, it is probably true to say, was looked at with fresh eyes. Here, recognition of the exceptional charm of the Ante-room to the Court was one of the most striking results. It was cleared, refurnished with more appropriate pieces, and relit to create the beautiful little room which we know today.

At the same period the Company was fortunate to receive from Reginald Rivington the fine grandfather clock which stands in the north-east corner of the Court Room and the fire-screen in the Stock Room. Another outstanding effort of this committee, renamed the Arts Committee, was one for which Past Master Cuthbert Graseman was initially responsible. This was the realization of the period value of a set of sixteen stained mahogany Chippendale chairs and a Master's chair. Made for the Company in about 1750, they had been discovered in the attic in a dilapidated condition; expert advice was sought and the whole set, properly restored, is now a much-admired addition to both Court Room and the Ante-room. That particular Master's Chair is not the massive (and awkwardly high!) one used for Court Meetings, but is the smaller, and more graceful, one which has frequently featured in the official photographs of Masters as published in the Livery Lists.

Much was done in John Betts's time, as he expressed it,

> to put the interior into its pre-war state of quiet and dignified attractiveness—and the work goes on; but some problems will have to be more fully recognized before they can be solved. Ancient buildings are expensive in upkeep and even more expensive if not quickly taken in hand.

In this last sentence, moreover, he sounded a warning note for those who, not surprisingly, felt that with its new-found wealth the Company could afford to embark upon altogether more ambitious programmes in all directions. Inescapably, costs were already rising with the higher standards which had been set, and members of the staff could no longer be expected to work without regular salary increases.

In summer 1962 the official opening of the great new Ludgate Hill building of the Colonial Mutual Life Assurance Company, on our former land, took place. To mark our appreciation of the harmonious way in which we had been able to continue to go about our business and to 'live with' all concerned—architects and builders—during the massive operation around us, the Chairman of the Colonial Mutual, Lord Rathcavan, with architects and builders, was most appropriately invited to a 'small lunch in the Court Room'.

Another social event of a most enjoyable and unusual sort

that year was on the generous invitation of a senior Liveryman, Roy Pratt Boorman. As owner of the *Kent Messenger* he has considerable printing interests near Maidstone and being that year its Mayor, he had organized an exhibition entitled 'Caxton to the Present Day', to which the entire Court was invited, preceded by a splendid mayoral lunch in Maidstone. The visit had considerable coverage in both local and national press, serving to underline the great connection between Caxton's work and ourselves.

A heartening commentary upon the sheer success of the earlier efforts to make the Hall thoroughly attractive for 'letting' was its use, in 1962-63, no fewer than seventy-five times for other than Stationers' Company functions. The intention was that we should be as helpful as possible to our own people, those connected with the industry; to those City Guilds which had no Halls of their own; and to our local Ward of Farringdon Within. Exactly as hoped, the Hall and 'suite' were becoming sought-after as a beautiful, and now thoroughly well equipped, meeting-place for occasions of many kinds.

For 1963-64 there succeeded to the Chair the greatest Master of recent years and one of the most colourful, talented, and altogether able men to serve the Company in its highest office, John Mylne Rivington. His portrait, as stated, now hangs to the left as one faces the fireplace in the Court Room. It was characteristic of the warmth of his nature that he should begin his Record of the Year by writing:

It was for me a year of intense happiness due to the wonderful friendship and unfailing support which I received not only from the Wardens but from my old friend and mentor the Immediate Past Master, John Betts, and indeed from every other member of the Court.

(He also added to the customary tribute to the Clerk thanks 'for his never failing . . . solicitude for my comfort and welfare on our many nocturnal excursions together'—an amusing reference to the convivial evenings which may be spent by Master and Clerk in the hospitable surroundings of other Livery Companies.)

Like many of his generation, he had served as a young officer through the horrors of the Western Front. He was a qualified barrister, he had also run the Rivington educational publishing business for many years, and he had played the major part with the Clerk, as we have seen, in getting the Bill for the winding-up of our English Stock put through Parliament. Moreover, his ability to make a witty speech enhanced the exceptional qualities he brought to his task. With Eric Burt and George Riddell the writer had the privilege of being called into Court by 'Jack' Rivington and later serving with him, during one's 'Master and Wardens' phase, while he was still Treasurer.

His was an active year in many respects. The Stationers' Company School and its future status had been under consideration for some time because of the need to spend a large sum on new buildings. With the rapid scientific progress of recent years, the continual need to extend the teaching of science and to provide more and more laboratories and technical equipment (including a small computer), it was impossible for the Company, from its limited funds, to give assistance comparable to that available from the State. Accordingly it was arranged that responsibility for the buildings should be transferred to the Ministry of Education, which inevitably involved a reduction in the number of School Governors nominated by the Company. The connection with the School, however, would not be impaired and there were increased opportunities for the Company to assist it in other ways.

Acting upon recommendations from a joint meeting of the Strong and Sotheran Scholarship Committee and the Pensions and Charitable Gifts Committee, the Court decided to award two annual scholarships tenable for three years at universities or technical establishments, while continuing the grants to help boys going on to universities to buy books. Additional funds were provided for the purchase of more books for the School Library; for musical and dramatic equipment; and for various purposes connected with the School, important 'extras' which did not fall within the normal scope of the Ministry's funds.

It is difficult to list them here, but two examples may be of special interest: one was substantial help in the building of a new cricket pavilion; another was the Headmaster's Contingency Fund, which is held by the Company, but from which money can be drawn at any time without delay to meet some particular and urgent need in the School. An example of the latter was the case of a senior boy whose quarrelling parents decided to part just as their son was in the final stages of revision for his 'A' Levels. When, for a fortnight, he was most in need of undisturbed evenings in a stable atmosphere, his home was breaking up. On a phone call to the Clerk, then Patrick Wells, the Head was at once assured of a grant to enable that boy to be boarded in a good private home for the crucial period. A small matter, some may feel, but a total justification for that Fund and a great satisfaction to feel that we helped to save one promising student from an almost certain setback at a critical stage in his career. The Fund can also assist masters at the School who go on postgraduate courses.

Besides the usual distribution of prizes to the School in Hornsey Town Hall Mr Rivington arranged for the School Choir to attend the then annual service held in accordance with the will of Richard Johnson, at Hendon Church, in June. They sang also at the Ash Wednesday Service in the Chapel of St Faith, under St Paul's, and the Master introduced a new and much-appreciated feature for them—'sausage and mash' for their tea in the Hall afterwards.

Two important London trade exhibitions of 1964 were IPEX, the International Printing Exhibition, and the World Book Fair, both of which were readily supported by the Master, who welcomed overseas visitors to them at two separate receptions given by the Company. In each case the Hall was kept open on the Sunday after the Reception, to enable visitors to examine at their leisure the displays of our Registers, Almanacs, books, plate, and other treasures, arranged by Sidney Hodgson and his son Wilfrid. It involved extra work for many people, but the interest and enthusiasm of the visitors were ample compensation. This type of entertainment was one of the many justifications for our existence, and for the expense and effort which had gone into the restoration of our Hall.

The concluding passage of Jack Rivington's Report on his Year spoke for many in its opening words and contains other significant points of special interest here. He wrote:

To relinquish the chair must cause every Master pangs of regret, but for me those pangs were of very short duration, for within a few minutes of becoming a Past Master not only was I honoured by the Court by being elected Treasurer of the Company, but was completely overwhelmed to hear John Betts inform the Court that he was in possession of sufficient funds to enable him to commission the painting of my portrait . . . To have achieved this object must have entailed a tremendous amount of hard work on the part of my old friend John Betts, and his associates, and a wonderful display of generosity on the part of members of the Court and Livery. 'Thank you' seem such inadequate words to express my feelings, but they are said with all my heart. To be the recipient of so much kindness makes me feel very humble.

The successful portrait by Cosmo Clark, RA—showing the subject's famous monocle and bow-tie—hangs today as a fitting tribute to J. M. Rivington's drive and skill over the legal proceedings in the House of Lords which extinguished the English Stock; it also marks a most distinguished Mastership by a member of that family which at the time had provided the Company over 200 years with ten Masters and four Clerks.

CHAPTER SEVEN

Change and Reformation

WHILE, BY COMPARISON with the late 1970s, the year 1965 may be viewed as a time of ease and prosperity, it was then that one foretaste of future inflation made itself felt in the Company. A new rates assessment of City properties adversely affected the Halls of the Guilds, including Stationers' Hall. It was assessed at £8,450 gross with a rateable value of £7,013 against the previous figures of £2,320 and £1,544 respectively. This nearly fivefold increase upon their Halls was the subject of vigorous and concerted action by all the Guilds. After long negotiation our figures were finally settled at a rateable value of £6,013—a reduction of £1,000 on the first figure but still a savage addition to our running costs. There was far worse to come in future years.

More cheerful, in that year, was the imaginative establishment of a Travelling Exhibition (or Scholarship) to enable young men—and now women—with potential for leadership to travel abroad to enlarge their knowledge of printing and allied trades; nothing is better calculated to stimulate and encourage young people at an impressionable time of life than to see how their jobs are being done in other countries and to have the chance to establish business and professional contacts there. This is an admirable part of the Company's work and one can only wish that our funds enabled us to do still more in that direction: the impetus for the idea had come from the Livery Committee with its 'Trade Co-operation Sub-Committee' under Harold Underhill.

In this same year the writer, as a junior Assistant, had next to him in Court one of the two Livery Representatives, then

Christopher Rivington. Moments of ceremonial during Court meetings sometimes give opportunity for exchange of ideas with one's neighbours; thus it came about that above the signatures of the two of us there was circulated to members of the Court a confidential memorandum entitled *Election of Liverymen to the Court of Assistants and Election of Master and Wardens*. The essence of the three-page close-typed foolscap document—mainly Christopher Rivington's work—was that:

1. The Stationers' Company in contrast to most Livery Companies had at least three thriving trades associated with it, but now had a different role from that of the past because employers' associations and trade unions covered what had been its earlier operations.

2. We believed that Liverymen would welcome a stronger trade interest on the part of their Company, that more could be done if the Court desired it, e.g., more exhibitions, lectures, discussion meetings at the Hall; greater moral and financial support for training in the trades; entertaining of leading employers and trade unionists, etc. But to steer the Company back to nearer its old position at the centre would need strong leadership and that essentially called for a lower average age on the Court.

3. Then—and it is still true today—a Liveryman would rarely be called into Court until thirty-five years from joining, and he might become Master after about forty-five years in all. No one can normally be Master under about sixty-five and anyone joining the Livery over thirty years of age must be an old man when Master. Yet under the existing rules *any* Liveryman living long enough could become Master, thus making longevity rather than ability the prime qualification for the position. While in the main we had been lucky in recent years with men who had proved very active for their years, inevitably from time to time some found themselves in the Chair when, through no fault of theirs, they were too old for the job.

4. Without suggesting that *all* Assistants must be younger,

we sought to see a sprinkling of younger men and of those still active in corporate work for their trades. It was unfortunate that the Company was denied on the Court the services of some leading figures in the printing, publishing, and papermaking trades who lacked the necessary seniority, though they had served for fifteen years or more on the Livery.

5. A strong case was made for Selective Election to the Court in *some* form, granted always that such candidates should have one at least of the following qualifications:

    (a) Strong interest in and record of service to the Company.

    (b) High standing in one of the associated trades.

    (c) High standing in the City of London.

It was also mentioned that many other Livery Companies at that time had selective election to their Courts. The final recommendation was simply that as a first step the Court should set up a combined Committee of Assistants and Livery-men under the Chairmanship of the Treasurer, J. M. Rivington (who had shown himself in some sympathy with the ideas put forward), the terms of reference to be:

To examine procedures and customs for calling Liverymen into the Court and electing Master and Wardens . . . in the light of present and future needs of the Company, and particularly with reference to the Company's aim of being more closely connected with its associated trades; and to recommend what changes, if any, should be made . . .

The memorandum was circulated in January 1965 and it was October before the *ad hoc* Committee was appointed by the Court. Service upon it was an interesting experience, with the inevitable clash between traditionalist and reformer, but, patiently and greatly helped by the skill of J. M. Rivington, it went to work, conclusions were reached, and in April 1966, under the Mastership of Colonel H. A. Johnson, the Court approved (though not unanimously) the recommendations that:

1. The constitution of the Court be amended to allow, in addition to the twenty-five Assistants to be elected in accordance with established practice from senior Livery Annuitants, the election of a further five Assistants from Liverymen irrespective of seniority.

2. A Court Supernumerary List be instituted to which Assistants so desirous, or no longer able to attend regularly or carry out their duties to the satisfaction of the Court, may be retired without penalty or loss of rights and to which Assistants elected without regard to seniority, unless an Alderman of the City of London, will be temporarily transferred two years after serving the office of Master, pending recall into Court on obtaining the necessary seniority qualifications.

3. The ballot to be reintroduced for the election of Under Warden.

Though some distance short of the original objectives, this constituted a great step forward by opening the way to the election of five members on 'merit' and by encouraging the resignation of those no longer equal to Court duties. (It could be said, with humility, that first steps towards this reform had originated with a former Secretary and a former Chairman of the Livery Committee who were, of course pursuing, in the main, ideas ventilated long since in that Committee.)

Prior to this new Order the possible risk of having to pay a fine on resignation was naturally a deterrent to elderly, or infirm, Assistants, some of whom remained on the Court when they could no longer attend with any regularity. Thus was the way blocked for younger men. An early result of the new rule was transfer to the Supernumerary List, at their own request, of Reginald Rivington and J. Alexander Bailey. Not long after, in January 1967, there came the first election of one of the 'further five Assistants . . . irrespective of seniority'—an ideal choice which fulfilled all that was hoped of the new arrangements, Leonard Kenyon. As Director of the then British Federation of Master Printers, his distinction in one of our Trades was unquestioned but, standing at 183 in the Livery List, it must have taken him many more years to have reached the Court. In fact he served a most successful term as Master in 1975-76. The second to be so elected was Jack Matson, who was even lower in the Livery List at 250, so would have been unlikely ever to have had the chance to serve on the Court by seniority; with his wide experience as Managing Director of the Monotype Corporation he, too, brought exceptional business skills to the Company in most difficult times, first as Treasurer and, in 1976-77, as Master. As the present List shows, there are three more Merit men already on the Court and the average age of Assistants has fallen appreciably since that of even ten years ago.

A key point in the constitutional revision, the significance of which is not perhaps immediately obvious, lies in the reintroduction of the ballot for the election of Under Warden. For very many years, the candidate had been selected on seniority and from then on, barring ill-health, progress to Master was virtually automatic. In the discussions of the *ad hoc* Committee it had been made clear that the new procedure would *not* apply to existing members of the Court at that time, but only to those who were subsequently called—thus avoiding opposition to the proposal which might otherwise have been generated. To some it may appear hard, but from the foregoing the reader will appreciate that there were good reasons for this change. Membership of the Court is very different from that of the Livery and it is right that, after learning to know a man in the greater intimacy of the Court Room, his fellow Assistants should have some genuine right of choice as to who should go forward towards the Mastership.

A critic might argue that under the new rules and with the Court increased from twenty-five to thirty members, progress to the top for the average man may take yet longer than in the past; theoretically it may be so, although in recent years some have 'made it' faster than seemed statistically probable. Against this remains, as already shown, the great advantage of a younger Court, more of whom are closely involved with the active world of business and affairs, than was formerly the case.

These changes were effected during the Mastership of H. A. Johnson, who summed them up in his Report, saying that 'It is hoped that they will accelerate promotion of Liverymen into Court, strengthen the connection of the Company with the trade, and increase the efficiency of the Court.' A change of a different and minor nature introduced by him was the long overdue circulation of the so-called Court Orders to the Assistants some days ahead of the meeting. Formerly they had been read out—with some ceremony and certainly with admirable clarity by the Clerk, whether Reginald Rivington or Patrick Wells—but it had been a cumbersome and time-consuming practice, leaving little chance for careful consideration of the Orders by those present. Now, as with most organizations, one receives in advance what are in fact the Minutes of the last meeting.

Also in the same year the Livery tie was evolved with the help of the Livery Committee and it quickly proved popular. (Unfortunately, and surprisingly, for the few who sported bow-ties, including at that time Sir Guy Harrison and Jack Rivington, it was said that ties in that form—for some reason—used far more silk and the cost would have been prohibitive.)

In 1965 also, an unusual distinction came to a member of our Company when Liveryman Stanley Cohen was appointed to the important office of Chief Commoner of the City. In that capacity he acts as Chairman of the senior committee of the Court of Common Council and Leader of the House, generally accompanying the Lord Mayor on all important occasions, including foreign travel or civic and social events in the City.

Francis Mathew, who had died in 1964, had been Managing Director of *The Times* and the Stationers' Company was gratified to be approached by the sponsors of the Francis Mathew Memorial Fund for help in establishing a travelling scholarship in his name. After some discussion an arrangement was made with the Institute of Printing for the administration of the scholarship on a basis similar to that of the Company's travelling scholarship, but more recently the Company has administered it. It is an interesting sign of the times that the two awards made in 1977 were both to young women who, by their achievements to date and their plans for the use of the money, far outstripped their male competitors.

Two characteristic and imaginative acts of H. A. Johnson were first his presentation to the Company 'through my wife'— as he charmingly expressed it—of a reproduction of the Company's crest in the form of a lady's brooch, to be known as 'The Lady Brooch' and worn by the Master's Lady when acting as hostess. Secondly, he introduced the idea of a 'Livery and Ladies' subscription dinner for which, at the time, it was possible for the Company to present the wines and cigars, thus enabling the charge to be kept moderate. It proved a great success. Many will also recall proofs of his skill as a Kentish fruit-grower by the quantities of the most beautiful strawberries he sent more than once to Stationers' Hall that summer. He has frequently sent us splendid apples in the autumn.

At a Special Court held in May 1966, and in the presence of many members of the Livery and their wives, guests, and the City Chamberlain, Sir Stanley Unwin was admitted as an Honorary Freeman and Liveryman of the Company in recognition of his many services to the cause of British books and his British Council activities. By special arrangement, also, the Freedom of the City was conferred at the same time by the City Chamberlain. Held in the main Hall, the ceremony of the Honorary Freedom is an extremely impressive one which many present would not have had opportunity to witness before. Sir Stanley was the youngest son of Edward Unwin Sr (Master in 1920). He was an exceptionally active eighty-one at the time and it is known that the honour gave him very great pleasure. Afterwards Sir Stanley and Lady Unwin, with all the Company present, including a fine gathering of publishers and booksellers, were entertained to tea in the Court Room—the temperance principles of the new Honorary Liveryman being well known!

It was, however, a particularly happy occasion, marked also by the generous gift by Liveryman A. E. Peters: a beautiful illuminated scroll in a handsome casket, recording the presentation.

The cynic may ask what is the use of the Honorary Freedom and Livery. As with many good things in life, it has no monetary value, but it can give intense satisfaction to the recipient and it associates our Company for all time with many people of distinction in national life or in our specialized circle of the printed word. One is happy to remember that with the similar admission of Sir Basil Blackwell in 1972 the Company honoured two 'Grand Old Men' who had worked closely together, in their earlier days, for the cause of books, the former as Publisher, the latter as Bookseller.

A significant event of 1967 under the Mastership of Donald Kellie was the admission to the Court of the first of the Merit Assistants, Leonard Kenyon. It could be seen as an historic moment and, for the Livery Committee, the crowning achievement of over forty years' agitation; few, if indeed any at all, would now say that this change in the Constitution has not been wholly beneficial to the Company. Donald Kellie had another 'first' by being the only Master, up to that time, to attend the Annual General Meeting of the Livery. He was, of course, entirely within his rights and having earlier put in many years on the Livery Committee, he would have had a natural interest in the proceedings. Formerly the Committee was regarded, from the standpoint of the Court, as a somewhat conspiratorial body and it was pleasant to think that a Master might then be 'received' in a friendly spirit. He made a short speech, then very considerately withdrew 'in order that the choice and decisions of the Livery should be free and unfettered', then returned in time to hear the report of the Senior Livery Representative on the Court.

In the same year, a valuable change in the arrangements for the Chaplaincy was effected after the resignation of the Rev. G. H. Palmer. Since his residence in Oxfordshire he had been able to take small part in Company affairs beyond saying Grace at Livery dinners. It was then decided to invite the Rev. Dewi Morgan, Rector of St Bride's Church (regarded always as the Printers' Church), to serve as Chaplain for a limited period. He was able to attend most Court Luncheons and he also preached at one of our Ash Wednesday Services in the Crypt of St Paul's. It was a happy plan and the idea has been continued with those whom we may regard as our 'local' clergymen each serving two years, Canon Tydeman of the Church of the Holy Sepulchre, Holborn, then the Rev. Peter Lillingston of St Martin's Within, on Ludgate Hill, and subsequently the Rev. Percy Coleman of St Andrew's House. Each one in his individual way has brought qualities of interest and concern for us in our efforts to make the Company of some service to our generation. Ten years after, in 1977, Prebendary Dewi Morgan has again accepted our invitation for two years more.

In 1967 a major change for the future of the Stationers' Company School was indicated: the Ministry decided that it was to become a Comprehensive Boys School as from September 1967 and that the number of pupils would be increased to about double. It rose subsequently from 550 to over 1,300 pupils and involved the Headmaster in a workload, and in a level of responsibility, very different from that for which he had been appointed in 1962. One satisfaction to the Company was that the name of the School remained unchanged, another that extremely good work continued to be done, but its nature and the complexity of its problems altered greatly.

Five years later, a visit to the School one working morning revealed something of the scale of the whole operation. Besides his teaching the Head is involved in an enormous amount of administration and immediately below him are two Deputy Heads, each, as it were, responsible for a large school even if one considered only a half of the total. On the material side, anyone educated in the first quarter of this century is inevitably amazed at, and proud of, the extent of equipment available, including even a small computer, and proceeding to a language laboratory, art rooms, workshops, and seemingly facilities for the exercise of every sort of interest and ability. At the top level there was the proud record of regular successes in university entries, frequently some to the Headmaster's old college, Trinity, Cambridge.

But besides all this, there was the new phenomenon of immigrant children, of whom there is an unusually large proportion in North London. The three main groups, each claiming—for interesting reasons—to be superior to the others, are Asian, West Indian, and Cypriot, comprising a total of about 350 at the School, many of them unable to read English when they enter at the age of eleven. A well-qualified teacher of English is reluctant to spend time giving instruction in the first elements of the language, but the resourceful Mr Baynes found a solution in the co-operation of what the world affectionately knows as 'the Mums'. Good-hearted mothers of somewhat older children came forward to put in their half-day (mostly) to go patiently over the elementary intricacies of one of the most difficult languages in the world. Under the rules, since they are 'unqualified', though admirable at the job, they cannot receive payment. This, however, is overcome by providing these splendid voluntary teachers with their lunch, after work for the morning shift, or before in the case of those teaching in the afternoon.

This digression may perhaps be extended further by remarking upon the very good simple fare served at lunch. Though a table was kept for the visiting Master and Clerk, with Mr Baynes and one or two others of the staff, we served ourselves on the cafeteria principle and sat surrounded by the cheerful babble and vitality engendered by a crowd of young people. Naturally they had to feed in shifts and it was interesting to see the orderly queues for the next service, held up in the entrance corridor, under the control of members of the staff, resembling trains waiting at signals to enter a terminus in the rush-hour. Over it all there was this great sense of youthful vigour, ready to lark about, yet reasonably disciplined. One need scarcely mention the music of the School. Anyone attending the Ash Wednesday Service in the 'Ancient Chapel of St Faith-under St Paul's Cathedral' has ample chance to hear the fine singing of the choir, frequently accompanied by one of the boys at the organ. Prejudiced we may be, but it would undoubtedly seem that the original foundation of the School by our Company and our support of it over so many years have helped to ensure that it is a rather special kind of 'Comprehensive' today.

Though it carries us somewhat beyond the period of the rest of this chapter, it is convenient here to record other activities of the Livery Committee which stemmed from its Annual General Meeting in 1967. Fewer than forty had become the usual number present, nearly all of them members of the Committee; the whole Committee retired each year and was usually re-elected *en bloc* because, though in theory it was open to others to offer themselves for election, the only information supplied about the candidates for the ballot was the number of meetings they had attended during the past year! Thus the choice had become heavily biased in favour of the existing members and possible new candidates had become discouraged, with the inevitable result that the average age of the Committee had risen steadily. Whereas it had originally been about forty, it was now nearer sixty, and there were cases where a member of the Committee might find himself actually called into Court, on seniority, within a year of serving as a Livery Representative.

A measure of reform was due and on the recommendation of a sub-committee approval was given, at the 1967 AGM, that the main Committee should consist of twenty-one, including all the *ex-officio* members (Chairman, Secretary, Treasurer, Social Secretary, two Livery Representatives on Court, and one each from Livery and Yeomanry Stock Annuity Boards). Most important, also, instead of all retiring automatically every year, there were to be five vacancies only—those who had served longest. Thus new members were drawn in more quickly. At that same AGM, as mentioned, the Master Donald Kellie, and Wardens attended, the former addressing the meeting and stating that the Court wished, for the future, that the Livery AGM should be replaced by 'Common Hall'—a meeting to take place in the Hall itself. A Sub-Committee of Court and Committee members subsequently met to implement the proposed change and since 1968 the new procedure has been followed. It has become a full Company occasion, with Master and Wardens present in their gowns, the former taking the Chair for the first part, during which he and the Company Treasurer also address the meeting. Thereafter they retire, the Livery Committee Chairman presides for the rest of the business, and later all meet again for refreshments.

When the Committee pressed to have the Livery Lectures printed annually, the Court proved reluctant to incur the expense, whereupon the Committee had the inspiration to interest the Printing Department of the North-West (London) Polytechnic, who agreed to have it done as a project by their students, at no charge to the Company. Since that Department has been transferred to the London College of Printing, the good work has been continued by the LCP. Thus well-produced copies of every lecture become widely available and are regularly placed in our Library.

With increasing costs attendances at the once popular Livery and Ladies' Lunches had fallen by 1968 to fewer than a hundred. The charge for tickets had risen to £2.50; on the other hand, the Summer Champagne and Christmas Wine Parties at around £1.00 were thoroughly popular, with 200 members and guests regularly attending. (Both prices are now an astonishing reminder of the speed of inflation.) For some years past the Committee had been granted £100 per annum towards its expenses and found it increasingly difficult to contain overheads. Tentative and nervous approaches about the grant were made and the Master and Treasurer were discreetly lobbied. Things took a little time, but in 1970 the grant was raised to £150.

In order to remedy what was felt to be a lack of knowledge among Liverymen about the Company's affairs and activities, Christopher Rivington, Chairman in 1968, persuaded the writer, a then comparatively new Court Assistant, to address a meeting of the Livery in the Stock Room on this subject. One recalls a lively evening with many interesting questions, from which it proved surprising, and a little disconcerting, to learn that there seemed then a real difficulty in getting younger Liverymen to offer themselves for service on the Committee. Remembered still is the enjoyable little dinner to which 'the speaker' was entertained afterwards, at a nearby hostelry, by the Chairman and two Committee members. Nine years later it is distressing to learn that in subsequent years funds did not permit these modest dinners to be charged to Committee 'expenses' on such unquestionably business engagements. The Livery Committee has done much for the Company for little reward—apart from the odd glass of sherry—and much of the time its members have had to put hands into their own pockets. That increased grant was well deserved.

The enterprising idea of inviting our Patron, the Archbishop of Canterbury, Dr Michael Ramsey, to a Livery and Ladies' Lunch in October 1970 brought a record attendance despite a £3.00 charge. The Master, Major Eric Burt, received the principal guests and it became a Company occasion of first-class importance. Other notable Livery luncheon guests of those years included Cardinal Heenan, Lord Snow, David Attenborough, Osbert Lancaster, and Marjorie Proops.

The first appearance of *The Stationer and Newspapermaker* in 1970, as the next chapter shows, was the outcome in part of the Committee's pressure, as was the 'Trades of the Guild Committee', set up in 1973 under Leonard Kenyon to provide for informal discussions between presidents and chief executives of the larger Trade Associations for the industries with which members of the Livery are concerned.

So the Livery Committee has gone on its way: in some years occupied with but small matters, but from time to time achieving a genuine reform and always enabling Liverymen to be kept in the picture in a manner better than a generation before.

An account of the one and only Renter Wardens' Dinner and its amusing sequel relates to the Livery Committee and should be recorded here. When the Renter Wardens for 1968–69 were called into Court to be formally installed, the Master, as had become the custom, reminded them of 'The Orders, Rules and

WESTMINSTER LIBRARIES

Ordinances' of 1681 which charge the Renter Wardens with
providing 'a competent and sufficient Dinner for the Master,
Wardens and Court of Assistants and all the Members of the
Livery and if default shall be made thereof, shall forfeit and
pay . . . the sum of forty pounds of Lawful Money of England.'
As had also become the custom, the Master also advised them
that they woud be excused this particular obligation. The
Renter Wardens for this year, however, decided that it was
time that this ancient Ordinance should be revived, in part at
least. Bracing themselves for expenditure of considerably more
than £40, they therefore invited the Master, Wardens, the
Court of Assistants, and the Chairman of the Livery Committee
to dine with them in Hall on 18 March 1969. It was a splendid
occasion and carried out with full ceremony, the Renter
Wardens formally escorting their chief guest, the Master, into
dinner in the Court Room, fully robed and preceded by the
Beadle. During dinner, students of the Trinity College of
Music sang madrigals. There were, of course, toasts to the
Queen and the Master proposed the Health of the Renter
Wardens. This was seconded by the Treasurer, John Mylne
Rivington, who, with his great sense of occasion and gift of
humour, delivered his entire speech in verse. Unhappily, no
record remains of this bardic oration, but this was his letter of
thanks to the Renter Wardens:

Renter Wardens Dinner
18th March 1969

Wyndham-Smith and Lovett-Darby,
Mandl and McGarry too,
May I hasten to express
My most grateful thanks to you,
For the quite delightful thought
To give a Dinner to the Court.

It truly was a lovely night,
With every detail planned just right,
And everything so very good,

Such fragrant wines, such well-cooked food,
And what I'm sure we liked the most,
Such very kind and charming Hosts.

> J. M. Rivington
> The Treasurer
> 19th March 1969

One of the Renter Wardens happened also to be the Secretary of the Livery Committee, David Wyndham-Smith, and he replied:

Your letter, Mr. Treasurer, I will always treasure.
It will recall that splendid night when we had the pleasure
And the signal honour of entertaining you,
The Court and both the Wardens and THE MASTER too.
Your four Renter Wardens had a common thought
To express sincerest thanks to you and all the Court.
An ancient debt we too discharged to prove there were no
grounds
Why you, Mr. Treasurer, should fine us Forty Pounds.
So with expressions of relief and gratitude most fervent,
It is with pride and pleasure, Sir, I am your humble servant.

From that time until the sudden and untimely death of Jack Rivington in 1972, he and the Secretary of the Livery Committee conducted their correspondence with each other in similar 'poetic' fashion, which gave them both much simple entertainment. The concluding lines of the last in the series—a reluctant refusal of the invitation to the Summer Champagne Party—ran:

To your most kind Committee please convey
My thanks and my regrets, and also say,
Though absent, all my thoughts will surely be
With you and them on that most happy day.
Sadly your tickets I enclose,
Wet with the tears that trickle down my nose.

> The Treasurer.

CHAPTER EIGHT

The Last Decade

A NOTABLE EVENT in 1968 was the admission of our second Merit member to the Court, Jack Matson. Other references to him in this book leave no doubt about the successful working of the new system of election to the Court. Within the same year, 1968, another new Assistant was Guy Virtue, who also became Treasurer to the Company. During the very difficult time of rapid inflation the Company owed more to the skilled handling of its finances by these two gentlemen than many may realize.

The number of apprentices bound at this point dropped to only six, which resulted in the appointment of a committee under Sir Derek Greenaway to consider ways to encourage their number. The report which resulted brought some increase, but the numbers of Apprentices bound at Stationers' Hall has once again declined to a small trickle. No longer does one see that little pile of beautiful leather-bound Bibles and Prayer Books on the Master's table ready to be handed to the young men after they have been 'bound' (in accordance with the Luke Hansard Bequest of 1828). It is understandable that with so few printers remaining in London there should be this decline in their number, yet the traditionalist cannot but regret it. Some present in Court today would have had grandfathers, and in at least one case a great-grandfather, bound apprentice in Stationers' Hall. To that gathering of elderly men it was always interesting to witness the entry of present-day youth (usually well turned out, even if over the years his clothes sometimes became less formal and the order went forth that all *were* expected to wear ties!). The ceremony must have made an impression upon most of them and it did, of course, help to pave the way for later admission to the Freedom and sometimes to the Livery.

In 1967–68 the Hall continued to attract an ever larger number of organizations related to books and printing generally. The most important was the Reception by the Royal Literary Fund to mark their 150th year, which was attended by Her Majesty the Queen and Prince Philip, received by John Lehmann, President of the Fund. It was the first time in living memory that a reigning monarch had officially visited our Hall. Other functions were those of the British Paper and Board Makers' Association, the Co-operative Printing Society, the Amalgamated Society of Lithographic Printers (from Manchester), the Wynkyn de Worde Society, and The East Anglian Alliance of Master Printers. They were a varied group and each one must have felt that the Hall added greatly to the interest and attraction of their different occasions.

Our Charities call for special mention at this point. Partly as a result of the special allocation to our Charity Fund made after the sale of the Ludgate Hill property, and a scheme approved by the Charity Commissioners, we were enabled to increase the Company's pensions and make better provision for our grants to the various Trade benevolent associations. At the same time it was felt by the Charitable Trusts Committee that it was expecting too much of many of our pensioners for them to come to the Court each quarter to collect their pensions and that the money should in future be sent to them by post. Some of them in fact continued to come in person and they did undoubtedly enjoy it. Coffee and biscuits were served and every Master had always a friendly greeting and word of enquiry about their welfare.

For those who found it increasingly difficult to travel to Stationers' Hall—to say nothing of the mounting expense—it meant, however, that we were likely to lose personal touch with them. For this reason it was agreed to form a Welfare Committee of about eight Liverymen, each of whom accepted responsibility for four or five pensioners, visiting them at intervals to find out how they were getting on. Arthur Watts (who had been severely wounded in the 1915 Gallipoli campaign) was then on the Court and became Chairman of the Committee. He was assisted in particular by Hugh Dove, Thomas Avery, and Herbert Chappell, and together they did most valuable work. While it was not that many of the pensioners were in serious want, there were frequently nagging problems where a small extra grant could just cover some unlooked-for expense, or assistance could be given in obtaining additional Social Security help. Above all, especially for those living alone, there was great gratitude towards those who 'took an interest' in them—so often at a time when their circle of friends had sadly diminished.

In 1969, further history was made by election to the Court of our, then, only lady Liveryman, Miss G. V. Woodman. Though married and with a family, she was known in her business and professional life by her maiden name—and to all her friends as 'Pippa'. Showing great ability as a young woman in her father's business, the Fisher Bookbinding Company, she rose in due course to succeed him as head of the firm. Not only did she run an exceedingly efficient bindery but, working for a large number of book publishers, as well as printers, Miss Woodman had very wide contacts and friendships throughout the Trades of our Guild. Inevitably some questions were raised in Court, years later, when Pippa Woodman's name came forward on seniority. Some wondered how the City would take to a Lady Master when the time came. For a number of excellent reasons the vote went strongly in her favour and for eight years the Court gained the services of a charming, shrewd, and most knowledgeable woman. Had it not been for her reluctance to accept the highest office, owing to the effects of an accident, she could undoubtedly have occupied the Chair with distinction. So the Stationers' Company could rest assured that its innovation had been fully justified, bearing in mind, however, that Gertrude Woodman is an altogether exceptional person.

A famous name was once more prominent in the years

1969-70 when Charles Rivington succeeded to the Mastership where six members of his family had preceded him during the previous hundred years. With a level of scholarship and of art appreciation not possessed by many Masters, he brought valuable gifts to his task. One of his innovations was the determined effort made to track down the hundreds of Freemen of the Company who had never proceeded to take the Livery and with whom we had since lost touch. Over 400 letters went out to those who had taken the Freedom in the past twenty-five years and of these about 200 replied. A proportion of them were invited to a wine party in Stationers' Hall, each one being offered the chance to bring a guest. A thoroughly successful gathering resulted and in the opinion of some it was an exceptionally happy and worthwhile evening. Many of the Freemen proved to be young men—not so very far beyond the completion of their 'time' as Apprentices, but already earning good money—and most seemed to bring with them an attractive young wife or girl friend. To have the chance to talk to them, find out something of their present jobs, and show them the beauties of the Hall and Court Room was extremely rewarding and one could feel that genuine interest in the Company was aroused. It is to be hoped that the idea may be revived in the future. Such a comparatively modest form of entertainment might be more widely supported and paid for by those attending than can be the case with a dinner. This is, of course, not to disparage for one moment the excellent Freemen's Dinners organized in recent years by Colonel Richards, but their appeal tends, inevitably, to be to a somewhat different stratum from that of the original party mentioned above. The need is to continue some effort to bring back to our fold the once 'lost' Freemen.

Traditionally, applicants for membership of the Livery had been interviewed by the Wardens who inevitably changed every year. To give more continuity for the future a Standing Committee of the Wardens, with Donald Kellie and Guy Virtue, was appointed to deal with such applications, and so that they should not be inhibited by the classifications of eligible and non-eligible trades as laid down by an Ordinance of 1961, a revision of an earlier one of 1949 was made. In its new form this provided the following guidance:

> That all persons engaged in the business of booksellers, publishers, printers, typefounders, papermakers, engravers, bookbinders and other allied trades, should be eligible as candidates for admission to the Livery of the Company by redemption, subject to the approval of the Court.

It stands as a good working basis for the Selection Committee, leaving it some useful latitude in the matter of 'allied trades'.

Another Rivington innovation was to organize the long overdue tidying-up of the attic above the Court Room and thus prepare the way a few years later for the establishment of the Company's Library, of which more is said below. He was also concerned to provide for the better use of the ancient shelves, or alcoves, at each end of the Hall—pointing out their value for display, for example for interesting books or other printed matter; otherwise visitors to the Hall might see no example whatever of our Craft. With a nice touch Charles Rivington observed that 'After all, books can be beautiful things in themselves . . . in this respect we are more fortunate in our products than, say, the Butchers' or Fishmongers' Companies.' He provided at his own expense proper display equipment for two of the alcoves at the south end, complete with lockable glass panels; these were later doubled by H. V. B. Dove. The idea was later extended at the north end of the Hall by Sir Derek and Alan Greenaway.

Efforts to make the Company of greater significance to its Trades were well exemplified by the use of the Hall for more than fifty engagements by various bodies during 1970, a state of affairs assisted by the excellent cooking provided by Mrs Millington, wife of our Hall Keeper at the time.

A further Rivington contribution was to revive discussion, begun earlier by Colonel Johnson, about the possibility of creating a private room for the Master above what was then a store room just to the north of the Clerk's office. To some it might have seemed impractical, but within two years, as we know, the scheme was completed to the great advantage of future Masters, the writer being the first one to enjoy its comforts throughout his term of office.

Previously the only direct access to the Court Room, from the Clerk's new offices on the west side of the garden, had been up the rather unsightly iron staircase and into the nearest french windows: adequate on a fine day, but not in wet or bitter weather. Replanning of the area with our architect, Mr Gurney, produced a convenient internal staircase leading up to an attractive room 'under the roof' of the old warehouse, but lit by two large dormer windows looking out upon the garden. Immediately ahead at the top of the stairs one conveniently enters the Card Room at the west end of the Court Room. For this there had to be an opening made in the seventeenth-century panelling, and on the advice of the Ancient Monuments Department we brought in an expert from Hampton Court Palace to show us how properly to do the job. The recommended cutting-through and hingeing of a section of the actual panelling has resulted in an almost invisible door.

For the Master during his year to have a private room, to which others do not come uninvited, is an immense boon not only for quiet discussion with Clerk or Wardens, but for work of his own and for selected hospitality before or after other functions in the Hall. One must add, too, that interest taken in the upkeep of the garden by members of the staff initiated by Patrick Wells, and the gift of tubs of flowers by Leonard Kenyon, have all added to the attractiveness of the outlook from that room. It is regrettable only that none of the Masters who had most to do with the conception and building of the room, Arthur Johnson, Charles Rivington, John Hubbard, and Eric Burt, were among those who benefited from it.

Several occurrences of special interest marked the years 1969–70 when John Hubbard was Master. First was the award of the Company's Silver Medal to Past Master Sidney Hodgson when he intimated his wish to be transferred to the Super-

numerary List. He had passed ninety years of age and the award
was a fitting, if small, recognition of his long and unique
services to the Company. The illuminated address presented on
that occasion read, in part:

> *Sidney Hodgson joined the Livery in 1907 and was called into
> Court in 1941 and now, in 1969, the Court—in recognition of his
> especial skill and knowledge and of his great work in keeping and
> preserving the unique and important archives of the Company—
> has ordered that the Company's Silver Medal be awarded to him
> and that the presentation should take place on Tuesday the 2nd of
> December 1969.*

Without the labour which that great Stationer had voluntarily
undertaken over so many years it is certain that our records and
bibliographical treasures would not be in the well-ordered and
accessible state that we know them today. The good work has
been splendidly carried forward by his successor, James Moran,
at present editor of *Printing World* and himself a bookman of
distinction.

Secondly, there was what John Hubbard termed 'the rare and
happy incidence of introducing a number of ladies to the
Freedom by Patrimony, which was initiated when I admitted
my own daughter as a Freeman together with the daughter of
Past Master Donald Kellie'. Subsequently other ladies have
been admitted to the Freedom, including Joanna Burt and
Judith Unwin, each one during the Mastership of her father.
For those who have no son it is indeed a happy way to perpetuate
some family connection with the Company.

A third achievement was the especial interest taken by the
Master in the restoration of the Past Masters' shields which
adorn the walls of the Hall and Stock Room. The project
necessitated much enquiry as to ownership of the shields where
identity had been lost and Mr Hubbard invited, where possible,
the families of former Masters to subscribe to the cost of
restoration. The idea was readily accepted and very great
improvement in this part of our decorations has been effected.

The Livery Committee also gave valuable help through their Chairman, W. C. Young, whose appeal to the Livery raised no less than £768.

Another innovation at this time concerned the traditional Richard Johnson Service. As many are aware, since 1795 and in accordance with the Will of Richard Johnson, the Master, Wardens, and other members of the Company have attended an annual service in Hendon Parish Church, on a summer weekday afternoon, to hear a sermon on the text *Vita humana bulla est* (Human life is a bubble) and to inspect his grave. It was a function which a few Court Assistants and Livery Representatives attended occasionally, perhaps out of curiosity—and, indeed, enjoyed the peace of the old Hendon churchyard as an oasis in the midst of modern bricks and mortar—but through the years attendance had fallen to a very small representative group of the Company. For them a coach had to be hired for the visit and, by long custom, the vicar's wife was put to the task of providing tea for the party. Master and Wardens reached the conclusion that it would be more satisfactory to hold the service in a City of London Church on the day of a Court meeting and arrangements were made for it immediately before the June Court, in the church of St Martin's-Within-Ludgate, which adjoins the south side of our garden. Assistants in their gowns form a little procession thither and the sermon— a different one each year!—on the time-honoured text is preached most skilfully by the Vicar of Hendon, the Rev. John Borrill, whom we subsequently entertain to lunch. Thus an old custom has been preserved in its essence, but changed to a form in which it can be observed economically and by a considerably larger number of the Company than formerly.

Another event of 1970, memorable for all who were present, was the deeply impressive ceremony of the 'lodging' in Stationers' Hall of the old Colours of 45 Commando of the Royal Marines. It took place in the presence of the Lord Mayor and Sheriffs at the Civic Dinner and involved careful rehearsal on the part of Master, Clerk, and the Colour party, comprising officers and other ranks of the Marines, to ensure that the elaborate ceremonial was carried through immaculately. These fine Colours had seen active service in Aden and elsewhere and they now adorn, and add great interest to, our Livery Hall.

Among John Hubbard's interests was old silver and he placed the Company still further in his debt, after his Mastership, by undertaking a major survey of all the Company's silver plate, of which a large quantity was entirely surplus to our requirements. Most of it had accumulated over the past century and there were more elaborate *jardinières*, rose bowls, and cups of innumerable kinds than could ever be used; there were also many odd quantities of spoons and forks which nevertheless did not make up sufficient sets to be used even for Court or Committee lunches.

The outcome of this survey by the Silver Sub-Committee was the considerable task of cataloguing all the silver, circularizing the Livery, and arranging for its exhibit and sale to the members. Every single piece of unused silver down to the last tea-spoon was disposed of in this way, thus ensuring that it all went to someone who would appreciate it for the association with our Company. Most satisfactory of all, a useful sum of money was realized and this was spent on the provision of electro-plate tableware of high quality for use at Court functions, in place of the hired cutlery and plate we had been obliged to use previously. Some argument arose over the replacement of old silver (unused) by modern electro-plate, but the latter can have a life of at least fifty years—probably more under our conditions of less than weekly use; it can be replated when worn and the table-setting of our smaller Lunches and Dinners can now present a much more distinguished appearance.

Two more years went by to 1972 when the Masters, Eric Burt and the writer, found their time very fully occupied, but the general pattern of Company activity was not greatly changed. Our income proved sufficient for our needs, care was vital, but there was no anxiety; fees were still paid for attendance at Court meetings and for all Committees relating to the Court such as Master and Wardens, Finance, and Charity

Committees. The receipt of the modest payments gave satisfaction to the recipients, disproportionate perhaps, but real, and especially so to retired members whose travel expenses for a special visit to London were thereby covered. Still more important, we had our free Livery Dinners and, in the case of Court Assistants, the privilege of inviting a guest without charge.

A 'cloud the size of a man's hand' became visible on our horizon, however, when in 1972 our accountants were asked to prepare a summary of our receipts and expenditure for each of the past five years. It was then found that the steady rise in our income, year by year, resulting from the major part of our investments held in equities, had done no more than keep pace with the inescapable rise in our expenditure. Though every item was carefully scrutinized and no opportunity, we then considered, was overlooked in the search for economy, proper provision had to be made for fair increases in staff salaries and pensions, while costs of repairs and catering inevitably moved upwards. Essentially we had to regard ourselves as living on a fixed income and it was difficult to contemplate any expansions of our activities unless they could be self-supporting. At least we were acting prudently, but few would have believed five years ago how many further economies would become inescapable in the near future.

In that same year, however, our Hall attracted the attention of film and broadcasting organizations. It was used first for a scene in a film entitled *The Ruling Class*, to provide the appropriate setting for an imaginary City Livery Company. Strict precautions were taken to ensure compensation for any damage which might be done and the battery of powerful lights, cameras, and technical equipment of all kinds appeared formidable to the layman. Our conditions were scrupulously observed by the hirers and no harm was done, while a very substantial fee was paid. Another use was for the making of a commercial film for the advertising of tea. One of us, curious to see what they were up to while the film was being shot, tiptoed to the steps leading down to the Hall just in time to see an imposingly gowned figure—as of another imaginary Livery Company—rise at the head of the well-laden dinner table and announce to the diners in ringing tones: 'Gentlemen, the toast is—Lyons' tea'! At least it provided a useful quip for the next after-dinner speech and the money, as indicated, was very good.

A more fitting use of the Hall, this time by the BBC, was in the spring of 1973 when the Amadeus String Quartet gave a broadcast recital there, mainly of the works of Mozart. Ten tickets only could be offered to the Company and Master. Past Master, Wardens, and Treasurer must be forgiven for feeling that, with their wives, they might reasonably allot the tickets to themselves. It was an unforgettable evening: the performers occupied a special stage in the middle of the Hall, one could see them at the distance of but ten feet or so, and the accoustics were perfect. Many Stationers could feel proud of the beautiful background to that BBC 2 Programme as it appeared on their TV screens on a Sunday evening some weeks later.

These special and profitable uses of our Hall were not forgotten when, within a few years, we had need to increase our income by all possible means.

Consideration of the Copyright Registry, the amount of clerical work involved, and the time of our staff occupied on it showed justification for a substantial increase in the fees charged both for the actual 'Entering' and for the certified copy of the Entry. Since it was mainly for commercial purposes that our Registration was sought, there seemed no reason to anticipate any objection to a higher scale, and so it proved. The number of applicants has remained constant and our receipts have risen to over £1,000 per annum.

Efforts to make the fullest possible use of all our premises led to clearance of unwanted records and other lumber from the basement under the Hall. Then space became available, which the skill of our architect, Mr Gurney, converted into offices for himself, thus providing another useful addition to our income, one, moreover, capable of useful growth, as the rent is subject to regular review.

At this time a Sub-Committee under Leonard Kenyon did valuable research into the State Barges of the Company, which led to the publication of the excellent and well-illustrated book on the subject. It was written by Michael Osborne, son of our former Beadle and latterly Assistant Clerk, Stanley Osborne.

In his Report for 1971-72 Major Eric Burt made special reference to the 'splendid work and loyalty of the Livery Committee which added so much in the service of the Company, and he particularly commended the Livery Luncheon to which our Patron Archbishop Ramsey had been invited. The idea was entirely that of the Committee and the ease and polish of Dr Ramsey's delivery as he spoke on 'The Life and Work of the Archbishop of Canterbury' was a delight to his listeners.

In that year also, stemming from the Committee, came the appointment by the Court of an Editorial Committee to supervise the production and publication of *The Stationer and Newspapermaker*. Several numbers of this small periodical have now appeared and it has undoubtedly achieved its aim of giving regular information, and often pictorial record, of our activities to the Livery. Major Pratt Boorman, owner of the *Kent Messenger*, was the first Chairman of the Committee and he did much to establish it as a going concern as well as contributing generously, through his extensive printing interests, towards the costs of its production. We were particularly indebted to him also for sending his press photographers to cover many Company functions at that time.

One cannot mention the name of Pratt Boorman without recalling the splendid outings which the Court has enjoyed on his invitation more than once into his native Kent. His mayoralty of Maidstone and a Caxton Exhibition at Tenterden in 1976 each seemed to furnish excuse for the kind provision of a private coach from Stationers' Hall (equipped for the supply of coffee while crossing London Bridge and other beverages when oast houses came in sight); a good lunch with local dignitaries would be followed by tea provided by Mrs Pratt Boorman at their beautiful home, Bilsington Priory. Though serving on the Court for several years, our host felt unable to accept election as Under Warden and, to the regret of many, he asked to be transferred to the Supernumerary List in 1972.

Another famous name in Company records reappeared in 1974 when Alan Greenaway became Master; in accordance with long practice he had been invited to join the Court in 1964, ahead of his seniority, when he became an Alderman of the City of London, and ten years later he occupied the Master's Chair, as had his grandfather Daniel in 1911 and his father Sir Percy in 1933. Alan Greenaway and his brother Sir Derek, who followed him as Master, were both generous in their gifts to the Company. The former undertook the complete re-decoration and refurnishing of the Master's room on the floor above the Stock Room. This has been invaluable over many years, enabling a Master to keep evening clothes there if he wished, to bath and change in comfort before evening functions, and of course to sleep there and avoid late journeys home if he lives outside London. The donors also included extension of the idea begun by Charles Rivington, this now being conversion of the remaining 'Court Buffets' in the Hall into display cabinets, providing full security for the permanent exhibition of valuable pieces of the Company's silver.

Golf-playing members also are much indebted to Alan Greenaway for the formation of a Golfing Society within the Company, for which he presented the prize of a gold and silver salver in 1974. Before this the Company had, for a number of years, entered a team for the Prince Arthur Golf Cup Competition, an annual event among the Livery Companies, and on more than one occasion the Stationers' team was successful in winning this handsome trophy.

In 1971, following a survey of the entire premises undertaken by Dr George Riddell and Alan Greenaway while they were Wardens, the decision was taken to put to better use the extensive attic above the Court Room. Lumber was cleared from it and, largely on Charles Rivington's initiative, about half the space was equipped as a library. Both he and James Moran, our Honorary Archivist, put in a great deal of work, securing registration of the Library as an Educational Charity, attending to the furnishing, and fitting it out with shelving suitable for works of reference. For the present, concentration is upon the history and records of the Stationers' Company, histories, biographies, and bibliographies of individuals, firms, and companies engaged in printing, publishing, and allied trades, and also histories of other Livery Companies and 'other books relating thereto'. For a start we already possessed a nucleus of such books, though ill-arranged, but since the proper establishment of the Library has been made widely known to the Livery, and to appropriate firms, many more books have been offered. It is clear that our Library will become a valuable source for research and a place for the conservation of books on our specialities.

Fruits of the Livery Committee's earlier inspiration continued through these years with a succession of Annual Lectures. These were organized by the Publicity and Livery Lecture Sub-Committee set up by the Court and they covered various aspects of our Trades, as may be seen from the Appendix. The Lectures now quite clearly occupy an important place in the calendar of many and each one is printed afterwards by students of the London College of Printing.

Patrick Wells, who had served us ably and with courtesy and good humour since 1957, indicated in 1974 that he would not seek election after that year. With his retirement the Company lost not only an outstanding personality but one who had achieved an enormous amount for us over seventeen years of unprecedented change and increased activity. Through his life-long connections in the City and his membership of the Clerks' Association he had done much to widen the circle of those who regularly hired the Hall; he introduced invaluable professional advisers for certain of our problems; and, incidentally, he achieved the very remarkable record of 100 per cent attendance at the office throughout the years of his appointment. He was made 'Clerk Emeritus' for the months during which he over-lapped with his successor and was granted the Freedom and the Livery of the Company to mark the Court's appreciation of his loyal and devoted service. The prominent part which Patrick

Wells played in the redemption and extinguishment of the English Stock remains a significant item in our history. Stanley Osborne, originally Beadle and latterly Assistant Clerk, was then above retirement age and decided to leave at the same time. He too had been a good friend to many Liverymen, and besides his scrupulous maintenance of all our muniments, and the patient handling of the innumerable enquirers for them, the main burden of the work of the Copyright Registry had been borne by him.

In personal terms these two departures came as a blow to many, but for the future the idea that a retired service officer might meet our needs proved exactly right. An excellent choice was made, during the Greenaway era, in Colonel Ralph Alexander ('Sascha') Rubens; he had served with the Sherwood Foresters in North Africa and Italy, being severely wounded in the battle for Campoleone in 1944. Thereafter a number of staff appointments had taken him to many parts of the world and he had ended his military career as Head of Management Information for the Army. His efficiency and the rapidity of his grasp of the world of City Livery Companies have been outstanding. Colonel Rubens has an excellent Assistant Clerk in Major John Moon, formerly of the Marines, and Dudley Ward, who came to us in 1971, has continued his good work as Beadle, ever ready to help with the unusual request in addition to his routine duties.

In these later years, so much nearer to our own time, it has not been possible to record so much of the activities of individual Masters, but it is an interesting fact that the first two Court Assistants elected on Merit, Leonard Kenyon and Jack Matson, became Under Wardens in succeeding years and thus followed each other to the Master's Chair in 1975 and 1976. Fortunately too, each was a chartered accountant by profession, in addition to the distinction and responsibilities of his career in the printing world; few therefore could have been better qualified to guide the Company through the storms of our worst inflation. Jack Matson had actually been elected Treasurer in 1972, on the sudden death of J. M. Rivington, and when the former was within sight of the Mastership, Guy Virtue became Treasurer. With our new Clerk these men were the architects of the firm economy measures which enabled us to remain solvent.

The pleasant little fees of £3 for Court and £2 for Committee meetings attendance were abolished in 1975 and all holders of annuities were invited to waive their semi-annual payments while, very properly, the Lunches for Court and Committees were simplified and cheapened, including even the drinks which preceded them. Livery Dinners had to be paid for and every effort was made to encourage further letting of the Hall while edging up the prices asked. Only our charitable and educational disbursements continued as before, and even with some increase. Fortunately the investment policy of holding approximately two-thirds of our funds in high-quality equities has provided a steadily rising income which, with the severe economies, has so far met our requirements.

CHAPTER NINE

Master & Wardens

MASTER AND WARDENS—that prefatory phrase to speeches, however brief, made in Stationers' Hall is a constant reminder of the true governors of the Company. They, with the Immediate Past Master, the Treasurer, and the Clerk, are the management under the authority of the Court. The system provides for constantly changing personnel among four of the members while ensuring that there is normally in each year only one completely new man among them. Treasurer and Clerk are semi-permanent officials, but, barring some accident of health, the incoming Under Warden progresses over four years to Upper Warden, Master, and then Immediate Past Master. During that time he is at the centre of the Company's affairs, knowing all that is going on, and it can be the most rewarding and deeply interesting of all one's time as a Stationer and Newspaper Maker. Happy the man who can so arrange his affairs that he is elected Under Warden on the day that he retires from full-time business or professional life! One still working full-time needs a good deputy for most of his normal tasks and, ideally, he should live in or near London, or at least 'have a foot in it' on most working days.

Since the 1966 revision of the method of election for Under Warden, when seniority has no longer been the sole qualification, the outcome is uncertain until the result of the ballot is declared in Court. The new Under Warden is then conducted by the Beadle to the far side of the Master's table to become a participant in the slightly complicated ritual under which three gentlemen change their fur-trimmed gowns while another,

123

the retiring Immediate Past Master, reverts to the rank of a senior Assistant, leaving his position two places to the Master's right, and goes to occupy the chair in the body of the room just vacated by the incoming Under Warden. The new Warden must be ready at once to address the Court with a few well chosen words of thanks after the 'acclamation' which will greet his formal presentation to the Court by the Master. Apart from, perhaps, a reply to his toast at the ensuing lunch he is then free of further duties that day, but for the next year he is 'two paces behind' the Master and then 'one pace'—watching closely all that goes on, and, unless he is very sure of himself, striving to memorize the many points of detail which require attention if Court business is to run smoothly and if he himself, when Master, is not to need promptings from the Clerk.

The new Under Warden who has had the good fortune in his earlier days to serve as Livery Representative will find especial interest in this further expansion of the work with which he has become partially familiar on the Court. Everything is now seen in greater detail; for example, all the financial aspects, income, expenditure, and investment, architects' and builders' reports on the care and maintenance of our ancient buildings, can be an interesting study in themselves. Associated with this aspect now there come proposals from the Arts and the Library Committees, each aiming for higher standards than we knew in the past, and School, Scholarship, and Charitable Trusts Committees also add their quota to the work.

Every Livery Dinner must be carefully planned, especially whom to invite as principal guests and which of them to be asked to propose the Company; it is now the custom for the Under Warden to propose the toast of the Guests at the Charter Dinner and May becomes his first trial as a speaker, before his peers, in the Hall. It is the less formal of the two main Dinners and the audience can be the more responsive. By the time November comes round, the same man is normally Upper Warden and he should by then face with increased confidence the thought of toasting the Guests in the presence of the Lord Mayor and Sheriffs. Beside these details there comes, of course, the delicate matter of the menu, the fine balance between cost and quality.

School business and the periodical visits of the Headmaster can make some of the most interesting occasions for Master and Wardens, providing sure evidence of the worth of our continuing connection with that now huge Comprehensive at Hornsey, which has been successfully fashioned from the Grammar School the Company founded at Bolt Court in the City. Most of the meetings attended by Master and Wardens are preceded, or followed, by a small lunch in the Ante-room to the Court Room and these can be not only pleasant in themselves but intimate and friendly occasions where, with the Clerk, confidences can be exchanged and new ideas explored.

The largest of such gatherings is usually for the Finance meeting at 2.15 in the afternoon, following the Investment Sub-Committee held at noon. Our investment adviser, Mr Philip Curtis, of Fielding, Newson-Smith, is always present for the Investment meeting and his expert survey of our holdings and of the world of business in general never fails to fascinate anyone who attempts to keep an eye on 'the market'. His skilful handling of our affairs has given us capital growth as well as substantial increase in our income which, though still necessitating strict economies, has so far enabled us to weather the worst effects of inflation.

Enough has been written to indicate the variety of experience which Past Masters have encountered, the many different problems which have faced them over the years, the skills which they have brought to bear for their solution, and the solid achievements which can be claimed. To end this brief account of the Company over the past sixty years it may perhaps interest Liverymen to have some outline of a typical 'Master's Year': it involves him in a greater variety of experience than may seem likely to those who see him only as an elderly figure at the Master's table in the Court Room receiving new Liverymen or giving 'the charge' to Renter Wardens and, of course, presiding at Livery Dinners.

Despite the two years they should have spent as a Warden most new Masters are aware that they must immediately preside over one of the most complicated Court Meetings of the entire year and before they have had a chance to feel at home in the Chair. And, incidentally, that imposing Master's Chair presents its own problems: so high off the ground that your feet dangle in mid-air unless you sit right on the edge of it, and you find yourself too high above the table for the usual reading glasses to focus upon papers at table level; some continually put glasses on and off, others use bi-focals (and at least one found comfort in the use of an old discarded pair of ordinary spectacles which focused about 6 inches further away than normal). It can add to the general excitement of a great occasion.

To take over an agenda half-way through a meeting is never easy: brief tribute must be paid at once to the retiring Master, with the promise of more to come at the following lunch. The Treasurer is usually re-elected then, with his Declaration to make, and there are some matters of routine business to finish off. It is wise to bring your own agenda paper to the top table too; your predecessor may have taken his off with him. A new Master is lucky who survives his first half-hour without some minor mishap in the procedures—known at least to the Clerk and himself if not observed by others—and he cannot but be aware that he is prominently there in the presence of several Past Masters who have all done the job before him. But to come safely to the end of that first Court, to be congratulated and greeted on all sides as 'Master', can be a most warming experience. By brilliant staff work, within the forty minutes since his election, the name of the new Master is to be seen already emblazoned in gold lettering upon the panel in the Hall as he passes through to lunch.

At the same time you become quickly aware that for the next twelve months you are rarely in a state of total relaxation at Company functions. No sooner is the Master seated at a Court Lunch in the Stock Room than the Clerk hands him the toast list for that day; it is difficult to do it any earlier because it is not certain who will be there. Some study of this is needed, as the meal progresses, in the hope that you may think up a complimentary, and entertaining, form of introduction for each one whose health is to be proposed. Then when the time comes and you rise with your 'Wardens, Aldermen, Brother Assistants, Liverymen . . .' and get through your little speech successfully, *don't forget* to propose the toast at the end of it, as more than one of us has done in his time; it can be the easiest thing in the world to do and can leave matters hanging in the air somewhat until some Past Master prods you into action.

Again, this first Court Lunch is additionally taxing for the new Master because he has to deal with an exceptional number of toasts: his retiring predecessor, now the Immediate Past Master, is the most important, followed by the two new Wardens and probably the re-elected Treasurer. There may well be a new Liveryman just admitted that day and the guest of an Assistant, so that a minimum of six toasts proposed and drunk is usual then, though, on a normal Court day, it should be fewer. Stimulating and enjoyable it undoubtedly is, but you are soon aware that you will be a different man, in many respects, over the next year, as gratefully you begin to install evening clothes in the Master's flat and take over occupancy of that comfortable office just above the Clerk's.

As I ventured to write five years ago:

From the moment when one is first addressed as Master and joins that long list of names stretching back to 1557 there seems to come strength, help and encouragement from many quarters. For this I do most particularly thank my colleagues the Wardens, the Immediate Past Master and members of the Court . . .

and as many other Masters have said, experienced support and good advice are always available. No man should shrink from the office solely on grounds of inexperience in such a position.

In the last month or so, before his election, every new Master begins to become involved with decisions on events which will not take place until after his accession. He is unlikely to leave the Hall on his first day without conference with the Clerk and there will be many days when he is on the phone to the Clerk, besides all those when he has to be at the Hall. To a surprisingly large extent he is constantly 'on the job', sometimes in correspondence with various Liverymen, and comparatively seldom is he free of the realization that there is another speech of some sort, proposal of or reply to some toast, which it would be unwise to leave just to the inspiration of the moment. For much of a Master's paperwork and for his meetings and discussions with his Clerk, the new Master's office is of the greatest convenience and a positive invitation to spend more time at the Hall.

For many years one of the first engagements has been the Livery Summer Wine Party, which provides an enjoyable time for the Livery to meet the new Master and his wife in an informal atmosphere, offering the maximum opportunity for personal contacts. An alternative, in less austere times, has been a Livery and Ladies' Dinner, and in some years the Freemen's dinner has taken place in the summer; both can be a great pleasure. At the latter, incidentally, it is customary for one of our Lady Freemen to propose the toast of the Master, a task invariably carried out with charm and aplomb.

One of the great rewards of the Mastership is the sheer interest and variety of the social intercourse, the many opportunities to meet more of the members of one's own Company—to realize how extremely kind people are to the 'Master and his Lady'—and the chances to meet the Wardens and Liverymen of other City Companies, and especially to see 'how things are done' in their ceremonial. Unless a Master is a man of iron constitution, he is probably wise to bear in mind that he will be making heavier demands upon his health, strength, and nervous energy than normal and here judicious use of the Master's flat at the Hall can ease the way for the out-of-London man. That said, however, it is so worthwhile to accept so far as possible every one of the invitations which come to him; many will be once in a lifetime and so frequently they show one some segment of life not experienced before.

We all know the *Wellington*, the ship for so long moored on the Embankment just above Blackfriars Bridge, but to be entertained in her at a reception given by the Scriveners' Company on a fine summer evening is uniquely enjoyable whether one is admiring the river view or the fascinating exhibits of the Company of Master Mariners displayed all over the ship which is their 'Hall'. Lawyers too, like doctors, make good hosts. We exchange hospitality with the latter, and dinner with them in the seventeenth-century charm of the Apothecaries' Hall, just off Blackfriars Lane, is not to be missed. It is likely to be an informal occasion, held after their early evening Court; their cellar is exceptional, speeches are short, but the conversation of medical men is very seldom dull. The Billingsgate and Leadenhall Market Committee one might not previously have experienced, but it invites the Master to lunch, in company with the Lord Mayor, in the interesting surroundings of Trinity House on Tower Hill and one is vividly reminded of two vital parts of London's trade. Still remembering the river, there is that wonderful ceremony of the Swan Dinner of the Dyers' Company, with attendants in the unique and colourful uniform and badges of those who participate in 'Swan Upping'.

Within a Master's first five months, but giving him time to find his feet, there comes the great test of our Civic Dinner in November. The most splendid function of our year, it calls up the full resources of Master, Wardens, Clerk, and all his staff: there are so many little things which might go wrong and which so seldom do, thanks to scrupulous attention to detail by many people. Two hundred handshakes can be quite an undertaking (especially with those whose greeting is demonstrated by exercise of the most powerful grip of which they are capable!), yet they remain a wonderful start to an evening—the sense of welcome to so many Liverymen, young and old, to fellow Court Assistants known for a generation, and to youngsters, there, perhaps, for their first Livery Dinner.

As the half-hour approaches and the decibels rise with the consumption of champagne in the distant Court Room, there comes warning that the Lord Mayor is about to leave the Mansion House. The Master descends to the main door under the archway and for once he may be glad of the thickness of his fur-trimmed gown. Few of us, unless we be Truscotts or Greenaways, can have waited there without at least some momentary trepidation, but soon the Rolls Royce flying the City of London flag draws up and one is happily greeting a man who, with his Sheriffs, almost certainly proves to have an ease of social manner which carries the proceedings comfortably along. So, up to the Stock Room, presentation of Wardens and Clerk, a sip of champagne, and by then all the other diners will be at their places in the Hall. The little procession headed by Beadle, Master, and Lord Mayor goes down the few steps into the Hall and makes its way to the top table, while the magnificently attired Marines band in the gallery plays the March from *Scipio* to the inescapable slow handclap of the assembled company. It is a great moment for any Master and he must feel proud indeed to view his Company and its Hall looking at its very best, the top-table guests resplendent in their official clothes, Mayoral and Shrieval chains and jabots, and the gorgeous scarlet dress uniforms of the Commandant General of the Marines and some of his brother officers. A Master may, or may not, be aware what food he is eating at such a time, but the toastmaster will in due course be hovering ready to prompt him to propose 'The Queen' (and, when the time comes, let him remember to pause just long enough on his feet to get that absolute silence which makes it the more impressive).

Over the coffee, three heads—those of Master and the two principal guests—are sometimes seen bowed over notes attempting to make last-minute adjustments to speeches, but first there is the Loving Cup, and a Master must remember that as he has to start *two* off upon their ways in different directions, he must himself drink first from each one. So come the speeches and some relaxation for the Master by the time he has safely proposed the toast of the Lord Mayor, the Sheriffs, and the City of London, and he can then enjoy the efforts of others. With astonishing speed, it seems, all is over, the Company bidden to 'make way for your Master and the distinguished guests', and he leads them out to the Court Room, warmed perhaps, in passing, by some friendly word of commendation from a seasoned Past Master on the success of the evening. Never does coffee taste better to some than in the cheerful atmosphere of that lovely Room after a Livery Dinner and it is the first opportunity which a Master has, during the evening, to mingle freely with everyone. All too soon the party is over— we can no longer afford to offer brandy at that stage!—and one can be thankful for the comfort of the Master's flat, the Hall now dark, and all silent save for the chimes of St Paul's.

Two special engagements of a Master's year are the Boar's Head Feast of our neighbours, the Cutlers' Company, held in December, when by candlelight choristers of St Paul's render superb carols, exquisitely accompanied at the piano by one of the Cathedral organists, and after it one may stroll quietly back to Stationers' Hall, perhaps diverging through the peaceful charm of Amen Court. The other invitation, especially attractive for lovers of church music, is the annual service to commemorate the Festival of St Cecilia, held in the Church of the Holy Sepulchre, High Holborn, on a November morning. Members of the choirs of St Paul's, Westminster Abbey, and the Chapel Royal—sometimes Canterbury also—provide the exceptionally fine programme in the presence of the Lord Mayor and, as those attending the service are mainly members of choral and other musical societies, the singing of the congregation is unusually inspiring.

Another great evening, free of responsibility for a Master, is the dinner to the Judges, given in our Hall by the staff of the Old Bailey. By neighbourly custom we grant them free use of our premises then, and it is doubtful whether one hears better speeches or enjoys more amusing company at any time during the year.

A Master often attends the functions held at the Hall by others and the Party given by the Royal Marines is outstanding. Every item of catering is, incidentally, done with the utmost efficiency by their own Mess staff, all food and drink being transported by them to the Hall. Ladies are invited and a Master and his wife are made to feel honoured guests for what becomes a wholly delightful evening. In many years, also, there has been opportunity for a fortunate Master to enjoy the altogether exceptional hospitality of the Marines to dinner at one of their Depots.

During the winter there is the Dinner of the Old Boys of the Stationers' School, with, later on, a luncheon, at both of which the Master must speak, but to a kindly and most receptive audience. School Prize-giving is somewhat eased since days when one confronted what seemed a gigantic audience of boys and parents in Hornsey Town Hall (itself almost the size of St Pancras Station), yet enormously rewarding if one had the luck to hold and to amuse them for a few moments. More seriously, one could not fail to be impressed not only by the great number of them but by the variety of race and colour represented in parents and children, sitting side by side and welded into one school through the genius of its headmaster and his staff.

The annual service for the Friends of St Paul's attended by Queen Elizabeth the Queen Mother, is followed by Her Majesty's visit to our Hall, as described earlier. Sometimes she is accompanied by the Lord Mayor and by the Bishop of London and other distinguished clerics: it is a red-letter day in our calendar and long may it remain the proud and happy duty of our Master to receive Her Majesty in this way.

One or two visits to the Mansion House are customary during the year and the Dinner given by the Lord Mayor to the Masters and Prime Wardens of all the Livery Companies, with their Ladies, is most certainly not to be missed. Also, should one have an eligible grandchild, in the right age group, the transporting of him, or her, in fancy dress to the Lord Mayor's Children's Party, held soon after Christmas, is well worth the effort. Centred on the great Egyptian Hall, with several side-shows, it is a triumph of the right sort of easy organization wherein children can quickly feel at home without getting out of touch with 'guardians'. A small part of a Master's year, but perhaps deserving of mention, as it is an afternoon to give exceptional fun to a lot of people, young and old.

With Ash Wednesday comes the ritual of the Cakes and Ale and the buffet lunch—another chance to meet Liverymen and Freemen—which has led to a larger gathering to go on to the Service in the Crypt of St Paul's than was formerly the case. A good preacher—often our Chaplain in one of his years—and the presence of the School choir give vitality to the Service, the Master's part being limited to the reading of one lesson.

The Charter Dinner in May is, for many, the most enjoyable of our major functions and one at which a Master may find himself with many old acquaintances from his own Trade among our guests.

The happiest evening and probably that of greatest ease will be the Ladies' Court Dinner, regretted only because it signals almost the end of the Master's year. There may yet be, however, another date which he will not easily forget. It is his privilege during the year to have free use of the Hall or any part of it for a private party of his own; food and wine must be paid for, the former hopefully provided by the Steward without need of an outside caterer. With family and friends it can be an evening long remembered.

These few pages may seem to indicate a continuous round of feasting, but this is far from the truth. Against some twenty to thirty of such engagements for the Master must be set a great deal of sober, hard work devoted to the running of the Company and the several aspects of its duties and responsibilities. Moreover, as Charles Rivington stated at the end of his Mastership, 'It is a remarkable fact that when one wants help and advice about some particular aspect of the Company's affairs there is always to be found some member of the Company who is not only willing but specially qualified to give it.' So, in these ever-changing times, the Company of Stationers and Newspaper Makers goes on its way, keeping up customs of unique interest and a Hall of exceptional beauty; its membership increases, though still confined to those directly concerned with the 'Trades of the Guild'. To them, as to numberless scholars and research students, the Company proves its worth and confidently one looks to its future.

Livery Committee Chairmen and Honorary Secretaries

CHAIRMEN

*R. A. Austen-Leigh	1920–27
G. de L'E. Duckworth	1927–29
*H. A. Cox	1929–32
P. N. McFarlane	1932–34
R. Metchim	1934–36
*S. Hodgson	1936–38
*D. F. Kellie	1938–40
S. E. Sandle	1940–44
W. N. Bacon	1944–47
*J. A. Bailey	1947–49
*H. F. Thompson	1949–51
*Philip Unwin	1951–53
Capt. F. A. Garrett	1953–54
C. de Ryck	1954–57
A. W. Last	1957–60
*Dr. G. L. Riddell	1960–62
H. W. Underhill	1962–64
A. G. L. Atkinson	1964–66
N. C. B. Harrison	1966–68
C. T. Rivington	1968–70
W. C. Young	1970–72
J. C. Moran	1972–74
Kenneth Day	1974–76
R. W. Read (*Elected at Common Hall* 1976, *called to Court before serving*)	
P. T. Rippon	1976–

HONORARY SECRETARIES

J. R. Riddell	1920–31
*G. L. Riddell	1931–56
C. T. Rivington	1956–66
D. Wyndham-Smith	1966–73
P. T. Rippon	1973–76
J. H. T. Perris	1976–

* Subsequently, Master of the Company

The Livery Lectures

1957	SIR LIONEL HEALD QC	Copyright
1958	SIR WILLIAM HALEY	The Effect of Television on the Crafts of the Stationers' and Newspapermakers' Company
1959	PHILIP UNWIN	Book Publishing Today
1960	SIR FRANCIS MEYNELL	The Typography of Advertising
1961	SIR JOHN SIMPSON CB	H.M. Stationery Office
1962	PHILIP G. WALKER	A Review of the British Paper Industry
1963	SIR JAMES WATERLOW Bt	Periodical Publishing
1964	SIR PAUL REILLY	Design and the Printing World
1965	SIR ERIC CLAYSON	The Place of the Provincial Newspaper in the British Press
1966	ARNOLD QUICK	Technical Developments and their Impact on the Printing Industry

1967	Maj. General R. C. Edge mbe	The Ordnance Survey
1968	Norman Fisher	The Printing and Publishing Industry Training Board
1969	Norman Collins	Colour Television and its impact on Printing, Newspaper Production, and Publishing
1970	Sir Max Bemrose	The Printing Industry and the Future: a Challenge to Youth
1972	Dr G. L. Riddell obe	The Printing Industry of the Future: its Technology
1973	James O'Connor	The Advertiser's Use of Printing
1974	Sir Robert Lusty	Books Today and Tomorrow
1975	Ray Tindle obe	The Press Today and Tomorrow
1976	Thomas Stephen Corrigan	Paper and Board Today and Tomorrow
1977	Alex Jarratt cb	Printing and Publishing: the Economic Future

Common Hall 1977

The following extracts from the Report of the Chairman of the Livery Committee, Peter Rippon, at Common Hall in March 1977, convey a good impression of the activities of the Committee during 1976–77:

This report must of necessity be somewhat circumscribed since the activities of the Livery Committee must be ancillary to those of the Company as a whole and we are always very conscious that it is our duty to be a subsidiary consultation centre, an unchartered sounding board and a generator of social activities . . .

Our year started in some turmoil because our elected Chairman, Raymond Read, was untimely ripped from us by his elevation to the Court and we were, therefore, faced with finding a replacement. Doubtless many of you are familiar with such a situation and the normal procedure is to fall back on a Pope John solution or appoint someone *faute de mieux*. I leave it to my Committee members both to interpret and to remark upon my analysis of their dilemma!

However to the year itself. Your committee organised social activities in the Summer Wine Party, the Livery Luncheon, at which we were addressed most entertainingly by Lady Isobel Barnett, and there was also the Christmas Wine Party. The Committee's brief for these functions is to provide opportunity for Liverymen and their families to meet in and to enjoy our Hall in the company of their brother Liverymen. We do not aim to make a profit but we frown upon a loss . . .

Other activities in which we were concerned were production of the Livery Christmas Cards and the leaflet *A Guide to the Hall* and the chief 'begetters' of these were Kenneth Day and James Moran, both former Chairmen, and now present members of the Committee. Mr Day has now taken over editorship of *The Stationer and Newspaper Maker* in place of another of our members Jack Cade, whose stint as Editor did him great credit. Mr Moran gained wide praise for his work as Secretary of the Caxton Commemoration Committee and the magnificent reception he organised in Guildhall will long be remembered.

During the year we were in constant touch with organisers of other Company activities and it is noteworthy that the question of making full evening dress compulsory for the Civic and Charter Dinners was mooted to the Court. Characteristically (also praiseworthily), the Court felt that such an instruction could be burdensome to younger Liverymen and the suggestion was rejected. Nevertheless the Court added 'Doubtless members of the Livery Committee could exert their admirable influence to see that full evening dress would be worn if at all possible.' That, gentlemen, I leave with you.

For the year in prospect, your Committee had hoped that we could have had a Silver Jubilee Dinner with a Royal Personage as Guest of Honour. This, however, did not prove possible as most members of the Royal Family are [this year] heavily involved with our fellow Livery Companies. Nevertheless, it has been decided that we should hold a Ladies' Livery Dinner on the usual date of the Summer Wine Party in July. The Christmas Wine Party will be held as usual in December.

In connection with the Silver Jubilee, I have been asked to commend to your attention the Jubilee Print Parade on Saturday 28 May. This is a combined Carnival and Sponsored Walk round the ten Old Gates of the City and the proceeds are being shared between the Printers' Charitable Corporation and the Prince of Wales Trust. Certainly this Company and our Liverymen should be to the forefront in this.

Well merited thanks to the Staff at Stationers' Hall and to the Officers of the Committee then concluded the Report.

Index

Printed and bound in Great Britain
by W & J Mackay Limited, Chatham